MAKE MONEY AS A LIFE COACH
2022

THE BEST GUIDE TO BECOME A LIFE COACH AND ATTRACT THE FIRST PAYING CUSTOMER

CONTENTS

INTRODUCTION

It took me five years to create a business I love, a business that allows me to make money from home doing work that fulfills me.

This may seem like a long time to you. For me, the time has flown by.

Along the way, I've learned who I am and how to run a business. I've figured out what I enjoy and what gifts I have. I've also discovered quite a few things that I don't like doing and that I have absolutely no talent for. Knowing these things is essential if you want to craft the perfect business — a business that reflects who you were born to be.

My Coaching Story

When I started out, I had no idea what my business would look like. I simply knew that I was meant to do something bigger, something that has an impact on the world, something that lights me up.

As I searched for my purpose, I learned about life coaching. I followed successful coaches online. I saw what their lives looked like. I was intrigued but didn't think coaching was for me.

I'm an introvert. As a child, I wouldn't answer the phone or talk with strangers. I still prefer to stand back and watch rather than be the center of attention. How could someone like me attract clients and serve them?

So I continued to explore other ways to earn an income from home. I was a stay-at-home mom and had no intention of returning to my corporate job. I had to make my business work.

Then one day I did something out of character. I sent an email asking if anyone wanted to hire me as a coach. This was unusual for me. I don't usually act until I have a carefully researched and well-thought-out plan. But in this situation, I knew that if I hesitated, I wouldn't go for it. I had too many doubts about whether I'd be a good coach.

And then a crazy thing happened. Three people took me up on my offer. Almost by accident, I became a coach.

That's when I hit a new problem. I didn't know what I was doing. I had no idea how much to charge, how to structure a coaching call or how to find my next clients.

I got lucky with my first three clients. These were people who already knew and trusted me. If I was going to add coaching to my business, I had to find a way to draw more people into my world. I also needed to learn about coaching packages, how to ask the right questions, and get a much clearer idea about the kind of coach I wanted to be.

I started down a long road of discovery. I read books, followed successful coaches and asked questions.

Eventually, I became certified as a life coach with The Life Coach School. But that came much later. When I first started, I didn't want to pay for an expensive certification. I didn't even know if coaching would be for me.

So I decided to keep offering my services as a coach and find my way through trial and error. This wasn't the fastest path to success. Finding new people to pay me to be their coach was not easy. And quite honestly, it scared me.

Yet, I followed through. In my first three months of coaching I earned more money working fewer hours than ever before. And I discovered that coaching was the perfect complement to my other passion — writing and publishing books.

I now have a thriving business. I write books. And I coach my ideal clients in my private (and free!) Facebook group. I am living my purpose.

Why Read This Book

Since you picked up this book, I'm guessing that some of my story sounds familiar to you.

You probably dream of becoming a life coach, or you already are one.

You may be struggling to find that first (or next) paying client.

You wish someone would tell you how much to charge, how to set up your business and how to market yourself — without spending hours a day online and without being pushy.

That's where this book comes in. This is the book I was looking for when I started coaching, but I couldn't find anything like it.

There are plenty of four- and five-figure coaching programs. But I wasn't ready for that. I wanted to test the waters first. I didn't want to make a big investment in myself until I'd established whether coaching was right for me.

One of my mantras is that clarity comes through action. You must take the first steps before you can know whether you're on the correct path.

This book will help you find that clarity. You will learn the exact steps to start your coaching business and find your first paying client(s).

I know this book is needed, and I don't want to wait before making it available to you. This is where my co-author, Melissa Ricker, comes in.

When I first met Melissa, she was already a certified coach and earning multiple four figures a month. In fact, she was also my first success coach, which means I can attest to the fact that Melissa knows her stuff!

To give you an idea of what effective coaching means, here are some of the ways my life changed when I started working with Melissa:

I set and achieved goals far beyond what I previously thought possible.

I stopped struggling to balance work and family.

I discovered what I most wanted and learned how to make my dreams a reality.

As my coach, Melissa created powerful and lasting change in my life. Wouldn't it be amazing if you could do the same for others? With this book, you can.

When Melissa agreed to help me with this book, I was ecstatic. I knew that together we could create a resource that would help thousands of people.

People who have a gift to share. People who dream of becoming the coach they were born to be. People like you.

You're about to embark on a life-changing journey — one that will transform you and the people you serve. It's an incredible feeling when your client thanks you for helping them achieve their dreams.

Getting the Most From This Book

This book is not like other books. It's not just a compilation of stories or suggestions. Nor is it a sales card designed to encourage you to buy a more expensive product or coaching package.

This is a complete success manual. It provides everything you need to start your business and sign your first paying clients. No more and no less. We don't waste your time with unnecessary information. And we don't hold anything back.

However, the words in these pages won't make you successful on their own. You must put in the work. Remember — clarity comes from action.

To help you take the necessary steps, we include Action Steps at the end of each chapter, so that you know exactly what you need to do and when you need to do it.

We recommend you read one chapter at a time. And when you finish a chapter, do the action steps.

Or, if you prefer, read the book in one sitting. Then go back to the beginning and tackle each chapter, one at a time. AND DO THE ACTION STEPS!

To further help you, we have also created a downloadable workbook and some other goodies to accompany this book. You can download the workbook and other resources from the bonus area here: sallyannmiller.com/coachbook.

If you apply the material in this book and keep going until you create the results you want, then success is guaranteed. The only way you will fail is if you take no action or give up before you reach the finish line.

Your Coaching Success

I'll never forget the moment I decided to write this book. I had just got off the phone with a client. We had been working on her business strategy.

During our call, my client had a breakthrough. She realized how she could free up more of her time and make more money. Her time was valuable to her. She had a young family and didn't want to spend her evenings and weekends working. This breakthrough showed her a way to solve her problems.

At the end of our conversation, my client said, "Thank you, Sally. Without you I'd never have found the answer."

For the rest of that day I couldn't stop smiling. And I knew I had to help others realize their own dream to become a life coach.

Now it's your turn. In the upcoming chapters, Melissa and I will guide you through the steps to start your coaching business and attract your first paying client(s).

Good luck and may your wishes come true!

Sally Miller

IS COACHING RIGHT FOR YOU?

The decision to become a life coach can change your world. When your alarm clock goes off each morning, you can barely wait to start your day. You discover a renewed passion for life and what you do for a living. There are no words that adequately express how you feel when you help someone move past a problem that has been keeping them stuck and causing them pain and anxiety.

If you are not sure whether to start your own coaching business, consider these two questions:

What if you had the opportunity to build your own successful business by helping others?

What if you could make a significant income by doing a lot of good in the world?

Well, that is what life coaching is all about.

But coaching isn't right for everyone. Not everyone has what it takes to be a great coach. So how do you know if it is right for you? First, let's look at what life coaching is.

What Exactly Is Life Coaching?

Every athlete knows the value of a good coach. In sports, a coach's role is to create a vision of victory for the team and assist the athletes to fulfill their potential in order to turn that vision into a reality. The coach trains the athletes by developing a strategic plan to enhance their skills. The coach encourages the athletes and holds them accountable for their performance.

Life coaching is not all that different. It's a partnership between coach and client that is designed to guide the client from where they are currently to where they want to be. A skilled coach helps a client identify the root cause of their problems and create change from the inside out.

A great coach enables a client to create a mindset of possibility where obstacles and roadblocks become necessary steps toward the achievement of goals, instead of stop signs. A life coach provides clients with an opportunity to recall the big picture and connect with goals while becoming more mindful of the internal resources they already have.

In short, coaches help clients live deliberately and with intention, move past self-limiting beliefs, and create a new reality for themselves.

Life coaches bring a profound perspective to their clients. As a direct result of this alliance, your clients will experience many benefits in their lives, including:

- Higher degree of self-love
- Increased self-confidence and self-esteem
- Improved consistency and momentum
- Greater clarity and focus in their true priorities and values
- The ability to balance multiple areas of their lives
- The production of rapid results

Sounds amazing, right?

Well, we talked about what a life coach is. Here is what a life coach is not.

A coach is not a friend to whom people vent about their problems. Coaches are professionals who empower their clients to create solutions to the obstacles they face. Coaches help clients define their deepest desires, recognize what is holding them back, and create a plan to move forward.

A coach is not a therapist. This is a common misconception. Life coaching is a unique service designed to aid people in the creation of success and fulfillment in their lives. While therapists and coaches both work to improve their clients' lives through positive changes, the process between the two professions is different.

Therapists focus more on past experiences and trauma, while coaches focus on the present and future. Through showing clients how their minds work and helping them unlock their greatest potential, coaches lead their clients toward a new future. Therapists dig into their clients' past to understand their present, while coaches identify current issues and work to modify them. Also it's important to note that coaches do not diagnose from a healthcare perspective.

Life coaches are as varied as their clients. Here are a few of the major types of life coaching, but this list is far from complete.

- Career Coaching
- Confidence Coaching
- Mindset Coaching
- Success Coaching
- Business Coaching
- Financial Coaching
- Relationships/Love Coaching
- Sales Coaching
- Executive/Leadership Coaching
- Productivity Coaching
- Health and Wellness Coaching

Why the World Needs Life Coaches

People hire coaches for many different reasons. They may want to change career paths, find their soul mate, get help advancing their career, lose weight or improve their health, determine their life purpose, start a business, or simply seek more harmony and balance in their lives. Whatever the reason, these individuals have realized they want to feel better in their life or career, but they don't know how to get started or how to get unstuck.

Everyone faces complex challenges in finding happiness and fulfillment in life. Even for those whose lives seem to be going as planned, they still may have a nagging voice inside their heads telling them there is a gap between where they are and where they could potentially be if they had the right tool.

Coaching is that missing tool.

We all need someone to talk to, an objective guide who can show us what we are missing. And we all need a strategy to get us from point A to point B. Without these things, people get stuck. They aren't happy and make no forward progress. Admitting the need for help and showing vulnerability is tough for many people. This is why coaching is essential. Coaching changes lives by unlocking true potential, true passion and true motivation.

It isn't just us saying this. There's data to back up our claims that the world needs coaching.

According to Marketdata, it is estimated that the US coaching market was worth $1.08 billion in 2017, up 6.5% from the previous year. The overall market is forecast to grow by 5.4% a year to $1.38 billion by 2022.

Further, in 2019 RealBusiness.co.uk reported that life coaching was the second-fastest-growing industry in the world, behind IT. The personal development industry was worth $11.6 billion and is expected to rise at a staggering rate of 6% per annum.

Benefits of Becoming a Coach

Life coaching is a rewarding career choice on every level. Not only do you forever change the lives of the clients you work with, but your business allows lifestyle choices that many careers never afford.

For starters, you get to be your own boss. Since you are the one running the show, the only person you have to answer to is yourself. Though be warned, you may turn out to be the toughest boss you've ever worked for! As your love for the coaching industry grows, you may push yourself more than any boss has ever pushed you. But this is an amazing thing because being your boss will benefit you in so many ways every day.

As a life coach, you can work where and when you like. Many coaches work from home, but you can work from almost anywhere. All a coach needs is a computer, a phone and an connection to perform all of their coaching duties. The options are endless.

You can set your own schedule. Do you hate working early mornings? Well, you don't have to. In your coaching business, you set your hours based on your lifestyle and personal needs. You can choose to work 40-plus hours per week (although we highly discourage it) or you can choose to work only two to three days per week. You are your own boss, remember?

You also determine your fee structure. You can choose what to charge your clients based on the outcome you provide for them and your income targets. You can set up one-on-one coaching packages, group-led programs or masterminds (we'll discuss more on this later) and charge what you feel your time and effort are worth. As a coach, you have an unlimited potential to make money.

Another benefit is you get to choose who you work with. Because you are your own boss and this is your business, you can be picky about who you accept as clients. This is not only a luxury, but it is also a responsibility. Your business's foundation is built around serving others. You need to learn who it is you offer value to and only work with those you can serve. We'll talk more about identifying your ideal client in Chapter Five.

Finally, your life changes as you impact the lives of others. The best benefit by far to becoming a life coach is the increase in fulfillment you experience in your own life as you empower others to become successful. Here are some of the positive changes you can experience as a life coach:

- You feel empowered to create the life you want for yourself.
- You become more connected to yourself and your inner well-being.
- You are inspired to get in better shape and enjoy more energy and vitality.
- You have a sense of purpose because you know you're helping other people achieve their biggest dreams.

Characteristics of a Good Coach

You now know what coaching is all about, why the world needs coaching, and the amazing benefits of starting a coaching business. But do you have what it takes to be a good coach? It is not enough to simply inspire others. Coaching also requires the ability to empower people. Coaching is not at all about you. Coaching is about your clients.

The end goal is to help the client identify and achieve their greater goals and live a more fulfilled life. An effective coach isn't out to "fix" anyone. A good coach wants to help navigate their clients toward designing their own compelling future. When people hire a coach, that coach should become the tour guide and allow them to define their dreams, recognize what is holding them back, and develop a strategy to move forward with clarity and purpose.

Before you decide to pursue a career as a coach, consider the following common characteristics of successful coaches and ask yourself if you possess these traits or if you're willing to develop them.

1. An immense love for helping others and a desire to do so. People come to you for help and support. If you don't absolutely love helping others, you will quickly burn out as a coach. Your business will likely suffer as well because people will sense your resistance.

2. Effective listening skills (including the ability to perceive verbal and nonverbal communication). The most important activity you do as a professional coach is listen. You listen to what your clients are telling you and what they are not telling you. You listen for clues and use those clues to help your clients move past their problems.

3. The ability to "hold space" for your clients. You are not your client's best friend or spouse. And it's not your job to buy into her story or confirm her point of view. Instead, you must show your client where her story is holding her back. Many people already know deep down what they should be doing to move forward toward their goals, but part of the reason they hire coaches is because they need that next level of accountability. Other people need you to reveal their blind spots to them. Your clients must know that you are there to support them, but that you also show them what they may be reluctant to

acknowledge. When they are standing in their own way, fail to follow through or fall back into old patterns, it's your job to lovingly point this out. This makes some people uncomfortable, but it is a necessary trait of a good coach.

4. The ability to recognize and articulate the strengths of your clients. A good coach can quickly pick out unique strengths of each client and build action plans based on those strengths. Two completely different people can reach the same goal in two completely different ways that are structured uniquely to the skills and talents they already possess. It is your job as a coach to identify those strengths and encourage your clients to use what they already have.

5. Empathy for others. Compassion and understanding are critical traits to have as a coach. You must truly care about your clients in order to help them achieve their goals. You must put yourself in their shoes and understand where they are coming from and where they'd like to go. Empathy is how you build deep levels of trust with your clients. At the same time, you must remain objective. This is "holding the space" for the client.

6. The understanding that coaching is a business and must be treated as such. As with all businesses, you need certain skills to start it, run it and scale it. You need to be organized and productive with your time. You need to be resourceful and willing to get help when you need it. You need to be professional and firm in your boundaries and client relationships. And you need to be persistent and dedicated to your business because starting a business is not for the faint of heart (and neither is coaching).

Action Steps

Throughout this book, we'll ask you to take action. We encourage you to complete these exercises because they will help you start earning an income as a coach. If you prefer, you can download a PDF workbook with all the action steps from the bonus area here: sallyannmiller.com/coachbook.

1. Determine which traits you already possess that will help you be a good coach.

2. Now consider which traits you might need to develop further. How will you develop those skills?

After reading this chapter, you may be saying to yourself, "I know I'll be a great coach, but where do I start?"

Well, we have good news for you! You're already taking the first step by reading this book. In the next chapters, we'll walk you through the step-by-step process we used to get our coaching businesses off the ground and land our first paying clients.

OVERCOMING YOUR FEARS

Before we jump into action, we need to talk about fear. How you react to negative emotions will influence your success as a life coach. And when you start something new, fear is inevitable.

Entering unfamiliar territory can be scary. Change is hard. You may doubt yourself and wonder if you have what it takes to build a successful coaching business. If you are experiencing self-doubt, know that you are not alone. We all struggle with fear. Even the most successful people are afraid.

However, fear isn't a bad thing. It means you are pushing yourself outside your comfort zone and growing. Your fear is a signal that you are on the right track. But you must know how to deal with it so that you don't allow it to hold you back.

We challenge you to lean into your fear instead of running from it. Confront it head-on. In this chapter we discuss a framework you can use to manage your negative emotions and fulfill your highest potential so that you can create the business you want.

Why Thoughts Matter

We start by examining how your thoughts influence your results. Imagine you're about to meet with a potential client and your main thought is, "I'm not a good enough coach."

This thought leads to discouragement. You enter the conversation from a place of self-doubt. Your words lack conviction. You fail to connect with your prospect. When you reach the end of the call, you avoid making an offer, or you do it in a tentative way. Your potential client senses your doubt and decides not to hire you as their coach.

Now imagine you have a different thought. Perhaps you think instead, "My coaching changes people's lives."

You feel inspired going into the call. You're excited to find out more about the prospect and explore the possibility of working together. During the conversation, you focus on the other person. You are clear about how you can help them and why they should hire you. You show up as your best self.

When you reach the end of the call, you make an offer to work together. You present your offer from a calm and confident place. The prospect feels your certainty and is eager to sign up with you.

In both these fictional scenarios, you're the same person. You have identical skills and experience. The only difference is in your thinking. Fearful thoughts create mediocre results. Positive thoughts lead to equally positive outcomes.

Below are some more thoughts which are poisonous to life coaches. Don't judge yourself if any of these are familiar. Even life coaches are human and subject to negative thinking! These thoughts are normal. We all have them. Judging your thoughts is just one more way for your brain to make you suffer. Instead, use the following as a guidepost to see where you need to work on your self-belief.

What if I'm not good enough?

What if my client fires me?

What if my client asks for a refund?

What if my business goes bankrupt?

What if I fail? What will other people think?

What if my partner doesn't support me?

I can't make a living as a life coach.

This is too hard.

I don't have enough time to build a business.

Marketing my services will make me look sales-y.

I'll never be as good as [insert name of successful coach].

So where do these thoughts come from? Why do you see the negative more quickly than the positive? And why does this seem to happen against your own volition? The answer lies in how your lower brain has evolved.

Where Thoughts Come From

In today's busy world, it's easy to move through life on autopilot — shifting from one task to the next without pausing to reflect on what you're doing or why. You are too busy, too caught up in day-to-day life to stop and notice how things are unfolding for you.

In this state, you aren't always conscious of how your brain is operating. You're letting it do its own thing without much supervision. And some parts of your brain have strong ideas about how you should live.

Take the amygdala for example. This tiny structure in your lower brain has evolved to detect threats and tell your body how to respond. From your amygdala's perspective, you're surrounded by physical and emotional danger. Your amygdala thinks unfamiliar situations could result in rejection by the tribe, or even death.

It works hard to keep you safely within your comfort zone. Your lower brain can have you reacting before you've even noticed what you're doing or why you're doing it. This can be handy if, for example, you're about to be hit by a car and need to move quickly to get out of the way.

But your amygdala can view all new activities, including starting a business, as life-threatening. If you let your amygdala and other parts of your lower brain run the show, then you'll spend your days on the sofa, eating chocolate and binge-watching "Downton Abbey."

The antidote is to build your self-belief. You start by observing your thoughts and feelings, and then learn to act on purpose regardless of the thoughts your lower brain serves you. Fortunately, there are other parts of your brain that can help you do this. In the next section, we show you how to harness the power of your higher brain to build your self-belief.

Stages of Self-Belief

Having self-belief means accepting yourself as you are. It does not imply that you are arrogant or that you think you are better than other people. Rather, it means you know that all humans are equally worthy — including yourself.

When you have self-belief, you do not need external validation. And you don't judge or shame yourself. You know you are already enough, and nothing can change that. There's not a single thing you or anyone else can say, think or do that can reduce your worthiness.

There are three stages to growing your self-belief and ultimately your success as a life coach. They are awareness, acceptance and action.

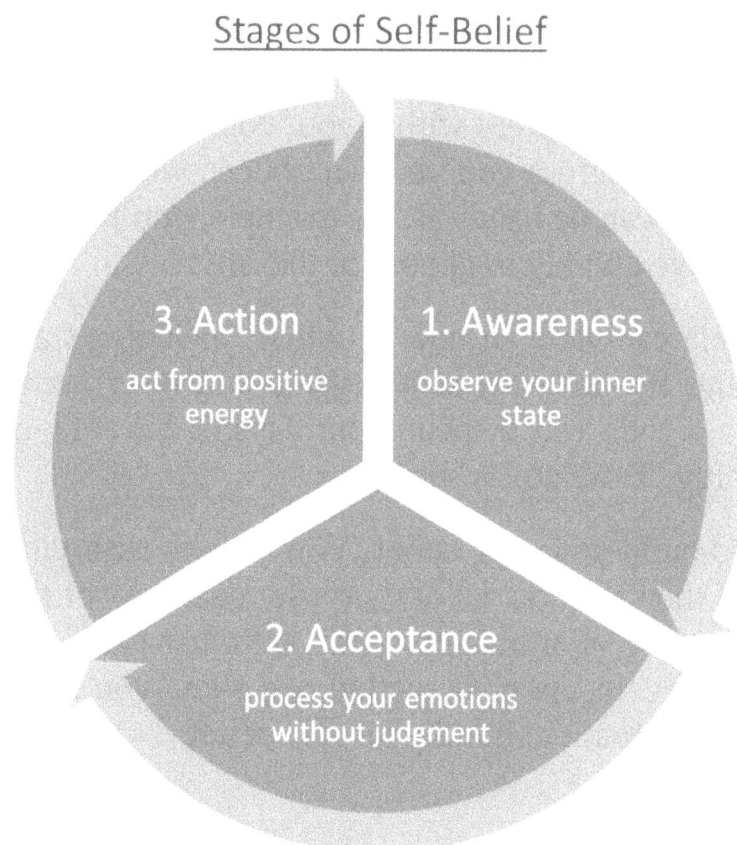

Stages of Self-Belief

3. Action
act from positive energy

1. Awareness
observe your inner state

2. Acceptance
process your emotions without judgment

Awareness

You cannot manage something unless you can see it clearly. You want to gain clarity around your inner state, which is comprised of your thoughts and emotions.

One way to increase your awareness is by journaling. Try writing about your thoughts and feelings every day, and especially any time you're struggling with a problem. This practice helps you step back from your thoughts and observe what's happening inside your brain.

Journaling is simple. There are three steps:

1. In your journal, write down all the thoughts and feelings you are experiencing. If this seems too overwhelming, start with a topic or question. Then write down all the thoughts relating to the topic or question. A topic might be "family," "money" or "business."

2. Once you've finished writing, reread your notes. Separate the facts from the story. Usually, there are few facts. Almost all of what is happening in your brain is invented by your mind. For example, "I can't build a business and be a good parent" is a story, whereas, "I have two children aged four and six" is a fact.

3. Finally, question whether the story you're telling yourself is serving you. All thoughts are optional and can be questioned. Remember, your inner state creates your results. Where you have negative thoughts, look for reasons why the opposite story might also be true for you. In the above example, you could ask yourself, "How can I build a business and also be a good parent?"

When you do this exercise, make sure you get everything out of your head. Don't censor yourself. Allow your brain to complain, clearly see the facts of your situation versus your thoughts and feelings.

Acceptance

Once you're aware of your inner state, the next stage is acceptance. Having negative thoughts and feelings doesn't imply there's something wrong with you. In fact, it means the opposite. You're functioning perfectly as an evolved human being.

Acceptance is knowing your thoughts and feelings are what make you human. They exist, and there's no need to judge them. Instead, see them for what they are, and don't let them rule your actions.

Accepting your thoughts and feelings means not pushing them away or reacting to them. Rather, allow the emotions to process through your body. This is a tricky concept to teach. The best way to learn is to practice it — over and over again. Here is what allowing an emotion looks like.

When you notice you want to avoid a negative feeling, stop what you're doing. If you've already started to react, then pause. Notice how the emotion feels in your body. Try labeling it. Is it fear, stress, anxiety or overwhelm? Describe the physical sensations. Where in your body do you feel it? Is it hot or cold? What color is it? Is it hard or soft?

Avoid indulging in your thoughts about the feeling. Instead, open to the experience of it. Process the fear through your body. The physical emotion is never as bad as the thoughts you have about it.

It can help to meditate or breathe into the emotion. Allow yourself to feel it, and don't be in a rush for it to go away. If you notice yourself reacting to or resisting the emotion, bring yourself back to the present.

If the emotion becomes too intense, you can also try observing it. This is a subtle skill that's similar to watching your thoughts. But instead, you are witnessing yourself experience an emotion. Your body feels the sensation and the higher part of your brain watches it happen. This can create relief while also allowing the emotion to be present.

When you shift into watcher mode, you're able to stay with difficult emotions for longer. You don't feel overwhelmed by the physical experience. As you develop this skill, you are no longer afraid of feeling your own emotions. You can process them instead of storing negative energy in your body. And best of all, you are willing to do anything — no matter what emotion comes up.

Action

The final stage of self-belief is action. Once you've accepted your inner state, you can practice taking action regardless of the thoughts you are having. You do this by acting from a positive energy and not a negative energy.

Most people act from negative energy. This type of energy is quickly expended and slow to renew. Let's look at an example.

Imagine you're working in your business and you are focused on external results: how many clients you have, how much money you're making or how many influencers you know. This is understandable; it's how most people operate. We live in a culture of wanting more: more money, more recognition, a bigger house, another car. Your brain's default setting is desire.

However, this wanting keeps you stuck on a treadmill because "more" is never enough. As soon as your brain receives one reward, it casts around for the next. The wanting never stops. You are acting from negative energy and it doesn't feel good.

So how do you get off the treadmill? The solution is to change the emotion or energy you're acting from. You need to switch from a negative action energy to a positive action energy.

When you're operating from negative action energy, you're attached to the outcome. Life feels like a struggle and you tire easily. Below are some negative action feelings. This isn't an exhaustive list. Your negative emotions may be different. Some of these feelings may even be positive for you.

Needy

Clingy

Grasping

Competitive

Envious

Convincing (especially when selling something)

Justified

Entitled

Eager

Determined

Notice how the last two seem like positive emotions. And perhaps they are for you. We all respond differently to the range of human feelings. Eagerness and determination are negative experiences for many people, because when we feel them, there's a tightness in our bodies. Our thoughts center around wanting a result. We find little to no satisfaction in either the process or the outcome.

The physical tightness and the attachment thoughts are all key indicators that you're in negative action energy. Negative emotions feel closed and constricted. In contrast, positive action energy feels open and expansive. There is no attachment. You feel more alive. You are living fully in the present. You are open to possibility.

Positive energy constantly renews itself, whereas negative energy leaves you drained.

Creative people often describe the experience of positive action energy as following their muse or being in a state of flow. When you act from positive energy, your experience and results are more satisfying. You enjoy the journey and create from a higher place.

Below are some positive energy feelings. Again, your list may look different from ours. The key is to notice how you're feeling when you're fully present in a task.

Accepting

Allowing

Inspired

Engaged

Curious

Enthusiastic

Open

Fascinated

Abundant

The first two emotions — accepting and allowing — are weaker than the others, but we include them because it's not always possible to love everything you do. Sometimes it's enough to accept the necessity of your work, stop resisting, and allow the present moment to be as it is. Flowing with life is much easier than fighting it or clutching at the future.

Action Steps

1. Find a quiet place and write down your answers to this question: "What am I thinking and feeling right now when it comes to starting my coaching business?"

2. Review your answer to question one and separate the thoughts from the facts. Avoid the temptation to judge your thoughts. Simply notice how the facts are few and your reality is being created by your inner state.

3. Set aside time each day to check in with the physical sensations in your body and practice processing your emotions. As you become more skilled at doing this, practice allowing negative feelings like fear, anxiety and overwhelm.

———

Okay, are you ready to face your fears and build your coaching business? In the next chapter, we explore the kind of business you want. It's time to get practical and start building a business and life you love.

DEFINING A BUSINESS VISION

If you're still reading, that means you've looked within yourself and made the life-altering decision to start your coaching business. Yay!

We're so excited that you made this decision. It will radically change your life. It certainly has changed ours. But now it's time to get down to business (pun intended).

The first step is to develop your business vision.

Why Visions Are Important

Visions are powerful. They can mean the difference between success and failure in both your business and personal life.

What is a vision? A vision is a clear picture you have in your mind of something. That something can be the way you want to look, feel or act. In this case, it's the way you want your business to look.

A strong vision helps you pursue your dreams with relentless passion and perseverance. A clear vision opens your mind to the endless possibilities the future holds. It helps you navigate obstacles and hold on to your dream even when the going gets tough. A vision creates your purpose and becomes a measurement for your future success.

Without a vision, you may not fully understand who you want to be, how you want to succeed or what you want out of your business and your life. You begin to lose focus, and you may throw in the towel at the first sign of resistance. Or you may end up going down a path you really don't want to go down and find yourself working too many hours in a business you don't love.

A vision is a mighty force in anyone's life, and it is essential for starting a new business. Your vision creates your target. And that target is where you focus your resources and energy. Creating a vision that speaks to you and your passions will help you guard your focus and grow your business.

The more specific your vision, the better for you and your business journey. This vision allows you to plan and execute to get your business up and running without wasting time, energy and money on the wrong things.

So many people skip this step and end up being drawn into information overload or sucked down the wrong path. They get pulled in several different directions, and their focus is split. Because they aren't clear on what they want their business to look like, they end up wasting valuable time and money on things that do not support their goals.

Now that you understand why it's necessary, let's define your business vision. Have fun with this exercise. And don't worry about getting it perfect.

You can always tweak your vision as your business grows. The idea is to get a clear image of where you see yourself going right now.

Define Your Business Vision

Your business vision needs to answer two questions:

1. What do you want your business to look like?

2. What are your business goals?

We start with the first question. When you close your eyes and envision your life as a successful business owner and coach, what do you see?

Here are some questions to help you define your vision:

Are you meeting with clients face-to-face or over the phone? Do you get dressed up to meet with them, or are you in your sweats? Are you using videoconferencing or voice?

How many hours per week are you working? How many days per week?

Where do you run your business? Do you have a home office? Do you work in the local coffee shop?

What does your typical workday look like? What time do you start and end? How do you organize your days?

How much money are you earning each month?

How many clients do you take on at one time?

Are you coaching one-on-one or in a group setting?

There's no right or wrong answer to these questions. The beauty of becoming a coach is that you get to decide exactly what you want your business life to look like.

Now think about the specific outcomes you want from your coaching business.

What are your short-term goals (one to two years)?

What are your long-term goals (five-plus years)?

How does your coaching business make you feel?

Your vision should be all about you and your life as a coach. In the next chapter, we will turn our focus to your clients. But for now, think only of you and your life.

The main purpose of your business vision is to outline your ideal business. If your business was everything you ever dreamed of, what would it be, who would you be, and how would you feel?

Action Steps

1. Answer the questions outlined above about your future business and life.

2. Now write a short vision statement answering the question, "What impact will my business have in the future?" Your vision statement will answer how your business will change the world. Think of it as your desired result.

Here are some example vision statements:

- Our vision is a world without Alzheimer's disease. — Alzheimer's Association
- No child in our city will go hungry to bed in the evening. — No Kid Hungry
- One day every person will discover his/her power to make a difference. — HandsOn Network

———

Congratulations! You've made some important decisions about your coaching business and the impact you will have in the world. In the next chapter, you'll learn why you should specialize and how to effectively find your niche as a coach.

FINDING YOUR NICHE

It may be tempting to open your coaching business to any and all clients. After all, why would you turn down anyone or exclude them from your programs? Wouldn't that be leaving money on the table?

Surprisingly, not at all.

Mark Victor Hanson, co-author of the famous "Chicken Soup for the Soul" book series, was qualified to write about any number of topics. But Mark knew the power of focus, and he became immensely rich by sticking to one specific topic. He has been quoted saying, "Pick a niche and grow rich." The words ring true with many career paths, and coaching is one of them.

Having said that, you don't have to pick a niche when you're first starting out.

Many new coaches accept a variety of clients before deciding who they most want to work with. In fact, some coaches will tell you that their niche found them and not the other way around. By helping a range of people who have different problems, they gradually home in on the type of clients they prefer to focus on.

However, you will eventually want to select a coaching niche. This can help you sign more clients and earn a lot more money as a life coach.

Let's pretend for a moment that you are suffering with a problem in your career. You can't figure out why you are constantly being passed up for promotions. After years of struggling, you decide to invest your hard-earned money in a coach. You decide to find someone who can help you advance your career.

If this is you, would you rather hire a life coach, or a career coach?

Most people would hire a career coach because he or she is specifically trained to help people advance their careers. Even further along those same lines, would you rather spend your money on:

A career coach or …

A career coach for busy working mothers.

Assuming you are a busy working mother, you'd probably choose to hire the coach who not only specializes in career coaching but also specializes in career coaching specifically for working mothers.

If people are going to invest their time and money in a coach, they want to know you understand exactly where they have been, what they are struggling with and how to overcome their specific struggles.

Not only do you get more customers and can charge a premium for your services by niching down to a specific market, but also you get more satisfaction from your business as the coach. When you are passionate about what you are helping your clients through — especially if you have been through something similar yourself — growing and marketing your business is effortless.

Choosing a niche can seem scary, but it doesn't have to be. In fact, figuring out your niche should be a lot of fun. It is a lot like self-exploration. You end up learning more about yourself in the process. You can change niches or further hone your niche as you get more experience, so don't let the fear of getting it wrong stop your progress or keep you from starting.

Having said that, though… we do suggest that you spend ample time in self-reflection before embracing your specialty and investing time and money in it. Give yourself at least a week to dig deep within yourself and find out what speaks to you. Don't worry — we're going to walk you through how to do this. There are six steps to choosing your niche.

Step One: List Your Skill Sets

Grab a pen and paper or open a document on your computer. We want you to physically list at least 20 things that you excel at. Yes, at least 20! That may seem like a lot, but once you get started, you'll probably rattle them off easily.

For example, are you good with numbers? Are you organized? Are you skilled at time management? Do you have a degree? Are you good with children? Are you a confident public speaker? Do you know the Bible from cover to cover? Do you love to write? Don't overthink it. Write anything and everything that comes to mind.

If you are struggling to come up with 20 different skill sets, take a break and come back to it later. Ask a few friends or family members for ideas.

When you're done, circle five skill sets in your list that you identify with the most or have the most experience with.

Step Two: List Your Life Experiences

Next, list the experiences in your life which have had a big impact on you, for example:

Had a baby in the NICU

Gone through a nasty divorce

Lost a family member

Been in a management or leadership position

Had a child with a learning disability

Completed an MBA or other advanced degree

Step Three: List the Wisdom You Gained

Next to each of your life experiences, write out the wisdom you gained through that life experience.

If you went through a divorce, did you learn how to hire the best lawyer? Or did you learn how to emotionally cope with losing someone you loved?

If you have held a leadership position, did you learn how to motivate your team? Did you learn how to interview for a promotion?

Try to list five things you learned through each of your experiences.

Step Four: Dig a Little Deeper

Before selecting the specialty that you build your business around and coach other people within, you should have a clear understanding of yourself. So let's dig a little deeper. Ask yourself the following questions and write out your answers.

1. What do the people closest to you say about you? How do they describe you?

2. What comes easily to you that you love doing?

3. Which of your skills do you perform almost daily without thinking about it?

4. What could you talk about for hours on end?

5. What do people say you excel in?

6. What is unique about you?

7. What did you want to be when you grew up?

8. What do people naturally come to you for help with?

9. What brings you the most joy in life?

10. What type of person are you most comfortable speaking to (e.g. women in their fifties)?

Don't overanalyze your responses. There are no right or wrong answers. Write down what comes to your mind first. The point of this exercise is to gain clarity about yourself. You'll also use what you learn here to refine your message. We'll cover that in Chapter Fourteen, so be sure to keep your answers.

Step Five: Combine and Create

At the intersection of your existing skill set, life experience, and wisdom gained lies the specific demographic of people you are most inclined to serve and the focal point of your business that will allow you to leverage what you already have.

If it doesn't come to you right away, give yourself some time to mull it over. Here are a few examples of niches to demonstrate that the options are endless.

Spiritual coaching for people dealing with grief

Financial management coaching for college graduates

Stress management coaching for executive level managers

Public speaking coaching for motivational speakers

Healthcare coaching for stay-at-home-moms

Relationship coaching for newly wedded couples

Work-life balance coaching for working mothers

Sex coaching for menopausal women

Health coaching for overweight teens

Emotional coaching for divorced men

These sound a lot better than "life coach," right? If you had a specific problem, would you hire someone from this list?

As you go through this exercise, you will see how your specific skill set and passions can be combined to create a thriving coaching business that has clients lining up at your doorstep. Get creative. The more specific your specialty, the clearer you are on your ideal client. The clearer you are on your ideal client, the better your marketing and targeting. The better your marketing and targeting, the more likely your ideal clients are to purchase your programs.

Step Six: Your Ideal Client

When it comes to creating a successful and profitable coaching business, there is nothing more important than understanding your ideal client. This person (and other people like him or her) is the person you guide and encourage through their fears, doubts and struggles. This is the person you serve in your business.

And coaching is all about serving your clients. It isn't about you or your accomplishments. It isn't about the money you earn. It is all about your clients.

So what does that mean to you? If you want to grow your business, you need to know who your ideal client is. You need to know what drives her, what scares her, what she wants most, her deepest struggles and frustrations, and how she thinks. Your ideal client needs to be real to you.

She is the person your website speaks to. She is your audience for blog posts and newsletters. She is the person for whome you write your advertising content.

As we already alluded to, if you try to coach everyone, you end up coaching very few. Once you've exhausted your immediate network of friends and family, you will find it difficult to attract more coaching clients without a clear image of who it is you want to work with.

You must be specific. Your ideal client should come alive to you. Don't worry if your client ends up looking a lot like you. Oftentimes as coaches, we are our own first client anyway.

Many coaches skip this fundamental step when they start growing their businesses. If you want a business with potential clients lining up to work with you, you need to first serve just one.

Answer the following questions to create your ideal client profile. By the time you are done, you should know exactly who you are talking to, writing to and marketing to. You should understand which information he or she seeks and what triggers him or her.

1. *What is your ideal client's gender?*

2. *What is his or her age?*

3. *What is his or her marital status?*

4. *What is his or her education level?*

5. *Does he or she have children?*

6. *What is his or her income level?*

7. *What are his or her hobbies?*

8. *What is his or her personality?*

9. *What are his or her personal goals?*

10. *What does his or her daily schedule look like?*

11. *What is his or her biggest source of pain?*

12. *What is his or her deepest fear?*

13. *What does he or she avoid facing?*

14. *What are his or her greatest opportunities?*

15. *What are his or her greatest hopes and dreams?*

16. *What does he or she hope to accomplish in the next year?*

17. *How does he or she like to learn?*

18. *What has he or she tried in the past that worked?*

19. *What has he or she tried in the past that didn't work?*

20. *What is he or she most grateful for?*

Action Steps

1. Complete steps one through six in this chapter. Spend time with this exercise (at least a few days), as it shouldn't be rushed.

2. When you finish, give your ideal client a name. Write up a short paragraph describing him or her and his or her life. Here's an example:

Tina is a working mother. She has her graduate degree in engineering and loves her job. After having children, she feels guilty that she enjoys her career. She wants to climb the corporate ladder, but she is afraid that doing so will affect her ability to be a great mother. She worries that she cannot effectively grow her career without sacrificing her family life.

Once you complete the above action steps, you're ready to start looking for clients. In the upcoming chapters, you'll learn how to package and price your services in a way that feels amazing to you and your future clients.

COACHING PACKAGES AND PRICING

Now that you have spent ample time in self-reflection and identified who you want to be as a coach and whom you want to serve, it's time to package and price your services. After all, as much as we're called to help people, this is a business. This part of the process can be uncomfortable in the beginning. But stick with us, because we're going to make this as painless as possible for you.

In this chapter we provide an overview of the most common coaching packages and pricing structures. Then in Chapter Seven, we guide you through a step-by-step process to define your first coaching offer.

When determining your pricing, keep the following in mind:

- The value of your time
- Your money goals
- The value of the transformation you are providing to your clients

This last point is the most important. As a coach, you change your clients' lives. Do not underestimate the value of that transformation.

We'll go through each of these pricing methodologies. We'll also give you some example pricing packages from coaches we surveyed.

The Value of Your Time

If you have a regular nine-to-five job or you have had one in the past, what is or was your hourly rate? We ask this because that number may already be in your head as the value of your time. But you are now running a service-based business, and the model is completely different. So forget that number. Instead, look at your monthly income.

For example, if you currently make $35 per hour at your job, it may seem like a dream come true to charge $100 per hour as a coach. But remember that coaching is not like a regular nine-to-five job. Coaching takes a lot of preparation and mental energy, so it is not practical to coach 40 hours per week. In order to coach 40 hours per week, you would end up working at least double that number and you would quickly burn out.

However, if your monthly income is or has been $4,000, and you are comfortable coaching 10 hours per week, you could back-calculate your hourly rate to be $100. With this number, you'll be in the ballpark of what you need to charge per hour to be financially comfortable, assuming that you don't want to scale your business. But please... keep reading.

Your Money Goals

In Chapter Four, when you created your business vision, how much money did you anticipate you would make? Your money goals also play a part in determining how much to charge your clients. If money is not a key driver for you, you may choose to charge less and serve those who do not have financial means to pay top dollar. However, if you have goals to launch a six-figure business and beyond, you need your pricing to reflect that.

Keep in mind though that your coaching fees are not your salary. You must subtract the money it takes to run your business. It takes a lot more money than you probably think.

Some typical expenses you might need to account for are:

- Income taxes
- Office supplies
- Insurance (medical, dental, life, etc.)
- Retirement savings
- Utilities (telephone, internet, etc.)
- Online expenses (website hosting, advertising, email service provider, automation software, etc.)
- Certification
- Continued education

The Value of the Transformation

Have you ever worked with a good coach? Have you ever gone through a significant transformation in your life or had someone help you solve a major problem? If you have, could you look back now and put a price tag on that transformation? Probably not.

If your marriage is on the brink of divorce, how much would you pay to save it?

If your health has gotten so bad that the doctors estimate you will die in less than five years if you don't change your lifestyle, how much would you pay for help from a professional?

If you have been unhappy with yourself for years, how much would you pay to turn your life around?

If your business isn't performing well, how much would you pay to triple your profits and scale your business?

Imagine if a client were to say to you, "I've made more progress in the past month working with you than I have in the past five years on my own. I would have found a way to pay you 10 times more if I had to." Why would they say this? Because the transformation your clients go through will completely change their lives, and to them… that's priceless.

When you price your services, take a long, hard look at the value of the transformation you provide. You are changing people's lives, and that is worth a lot of money. We talk more about this concept in the next chapter.

Resist Undervaluing Your Service

As a new coach, it can be quite intimidating to set your packages at their true value. You've seen the competition, and you may be tempted to set your prices low when you start out. You probably don't believe that people will pay a premium for your services. However, there are a few things wrong with this mindset.

Perception is reality. If you set your session price at $25, what perception are you sending to your potential clients? Most likely they will see you as a low-end coach who may deliver low-end results. Powerful coaching (especially one-on-one) delivers dramatic results, and your price tag needs to reflect that.

People are after a feeling when they buy something high-end. When they invest in themselves and purchase a highly personalized service, they are telling themselves, "I'm worth it." And they want that feeling. It's an important piece of their transformation. If your packages don't evoke that emotion, they may not be willing to pull out their credit card.

Your clients will put forth an effort proportional to what they pay. If you charge $25, how motivated will your clients be to put forth a valiant effort in your program? If they lose $25, it isn't a lot of money. However, the more your clients pay, the more effort they will put into the work because they want to feel as though they "got their money's worth."

Furthermore, your clients deserve you at your best. If your rates are low, you'll have to coach more people each month. This means that you will be stretched too thin to give your best to each client. But imagine how you would show up as a coach if you were charging higher prices. You would be able and motivated to perform at your highest level.

Coaching Models

Your pricing also depends on how you package your services. There are many options to choose from, and you may choose to offer several choices to your clients. We'll go through the three most common models and give examples of pricing based on our survey of practicing coaches. Then in the next chapter, we show you how to create and price your first coaching package so that you can attract your ideal clients right out of the gate.

#1: Individual Sessions

Individual sessions may be 45 to 90 minutes, but most are typically one hour in length. Rarely will your clients experience a dramatic breakthrough in one individual session. You may choose to offer these individual sessions as an option to someone who wants to try you out to see if working with you is a good fit.

In our survey of 10 coaches practicing today, the prices for individual sessions ranged from $80 up to $500. Your rate depends on your experience and your niche. The coach who charges $500 per session has clients in upper-level management positions. The average rate for individual sessions among these 10 coaches is $200 per session.

#2: Monthly Package

Monthly packages are popular because your clients are a little more invested. You need to determine how many coaching calls your package includes as well as what services (if any) you provide in between calls.

For example, you could offer a monthly coaching package that includes four coaching calls, a weekly action plan and mid-week email check-ins. When you have clients in your extended programs, you also need to set aside time to catch up with your notes and action items before each session. Account for all your time and set your prices accordingly.

Our survey revealed that monthly coaching programs ranged from $250 up to $2,500 per month with an average of $850. Again, the prices varied based on the coach's experience and the niche.

#3: Group Packages

Group packages are popular among coaches today. Now that most people have access to the internet, a portion of your coaching program can be prerecorded, and your clients can watch the lesson on their own time.

Another option is to run group calls. This model is especially applicable to the coaches who teach the same strategies over and over. In addition to the online portion, most coaches add in group phone calls, email support, Facebook groups and individual sessions (or a combination of these). Group packages vary widely based on what is included, the length of the program and the amount of time invested by the coach.

However, we recommend you start out coaching individual clients. It's important to build up your coaching skills. And the fastest way to do this is through one-on-one coaching. When you begin with individual sessions, you will also gain a deep understanding of your ideal clients and their challenges. This will help you create more effective and higher-ticket group offerings if you later want to scale your business. We discuss ways to grow your business in later chapters.

When it comes to choosing your packages and pricing them appropriately, there are no easy answers. You may need to spend some time in self-reflection to find out what feels right to you. Whatever you choose, do your research to find out what other coaches in your niche are charging. Look at the time you are investing and the transformation you are providing.

Finally, don't worry about getting it right the first time. As a coach, you can always adjust your prices later. The bottom line is that your coaching fees must work for you and your lifestyle, and you must feel confident about them.

Action Steps

1. Create a budget for yourself to understand how much money you need to bring in from your coaching business. Be sure to include business expenses, income tax, estimated Social Security and Medicare, estimated health insurance, and retirement investments. Divide that number by how many clients you'd like to serve each month.

2. Determine which coaching models you would like to offer in your business both now and in the future.

———

You now have a vision for your business and know what kind of coach you are becoming. You're set to build your coaching practice and start working with clients. Next, we go deeper into creating enticing offers. We will show you how to define your first irresistible coaching package, one that your ideal clients can't wait to pay for.

YOUR IRRESISTIBLE OFFER

Okay, it's time to put together your first coaching offer — one that's irresistible to your ideal clients. In this chapter we assume that your first offer is for one-on-one coaching. We talk more about scaling your practice and offering group programs in Chapter Fifteen.

Right now your goal is to sign some clients, create results for them and start earning money as a life coach. There are four steps to creating an irresistible offer:

1. Define the transformation
2. Describe your offer
3. Price your offer
4. Increase your prices

Let's jump in.

Step One: Define the Transformation

If you have just one takeaway from this book, then make it this:

People don't buy coaching. They buy solutions to their problems.

This is important. You must clearly define the problem you help your clients solve and the specific outcome they can expect from working with you. By delivering concrete and desirable results, you will create a coaching package that's irresistible to your ideal clients.

Start by thinking about the ideal client you defined in Chapter Five. What specific outcome or results can you help this person achieve?

Select one big transformation you can provide. Here are some questions to help you test your answer:

Is the result tangible and desirable to your ideal client?

Is it something you can deliver?

Is this something your ideal client is willing and able to pay for?

If you answer no to any of these questions, then go back to the notes you made in Chapter Five and refine your transformation. Here are some example offers from successful coaching businesses:

- Earn your first $2K as a life coach.
- Find Mr. Right.
- Lose 10 pounds.
- Publish a bestselling book.

Notice how these examples are both tangible and desirable. They are all transformations that the right people would willingly pay for.

Step Two: Describe Your Offer

Now that you're clear about the results you deliver, it's much easier to put a value on this outcome or transformation.

Imagine that you are your ideal client. This can be easy to do if your ideal client is an earlier version of you and has a problem that you've already solved. From the perspective of your ideal client, eager for the solution you provide, ask yourself, "What is it worth to have this problem solved?" Answer with the first number that comes to mind. If you're struggling to come up with one number, then it's also okay to write down a price range.

Don't overthink this step or waste time worrying about what other coaches charge. Also don't bother with the details of your package — we'll get to your coaching package soon. Simply focus on selecting a price or price range that's consistent with the transformation or value you offer.

Write this number down — this is the value of the transformation you provide.

Okay, you have an initial number (or range). You're now going to look for ways to increase this price. Think about how you can "up your game." How can you give your ideal client your best work? How can you change what you do and how you do it to ensure phenomenal results? What add-ons can you offer that will make your client's experience exceptional?

Example add-ons are: onboarding process (introductory resources, welcome email, etc.), check-in calls, email access to you, written or recorded coaching session reports, group support or community membership, training materials, scripts, templates and eBooks.

Write out all your ideas. Then come up with a new price (or price range) for your services that reflects the added value you can offer. This price should be bigger than the number you previously wrote down.

Next, define the details of your package. Some coaches start here. But this is a mistake. If you start by focusing on the number of sessions, your hourly rate, etc., you're not putting your attention where it's most needed. Whereas, if you focus first on your client, their problem, and the transformation you provide, you will deliver bigger results, win more clients, and charge higher prices.

Consider how much coaching will best support your clients in achieving the transformation you provide. Define the following details of your client package.

- Duration — number of weeks or months, e.g. three months.
- Number of sessions — e.g. six sessions or two sessions per month.
- Length of sessions — e.g. one hour.

Finally, review the coaching package you have defined from the perspective of your ideal client. Would they be willing to sign up for that level of commitment to solve their problem? If necessary, tweak your package until it feels right for your potential clients.

Step Three: Price Your Offer

You've already done all the hard work. In this step, you're going to pull everything together and commit to a starting price for your irresistible coaching package. Look at the numbers you wrote down in step two. Then select one price for your coaching package that's a little outside your comfort zone.

Now before you commit, make sure your price is realistic. When you start out, it's important to set a price that will allow you to quickly book your first paying clients. Don't worry, when you've gained experience and testimonials, you will rapidly increase your rates.

Review the starting price you selected in light of the following:

- Your coaching niche (what's normal in your niche).
- Your background and experience (think about your coaching and marketing skills and experience).
- The transformation you deliver.
- What's included in your coaching package.

Does the number feel realistic? Will your ideal client pay this price to work with you?

If necessary, lower your price. But make sure your final number still makes you a tiny bit nervous. When someone pays you that magic number, you'll push yourself to provide massive results. And massive results make for happy customers, glowing testimonials and repeat clients.

Step Four: Increase Your Prices

You're not going to do this last step straight away. Right now, your goal is to quickly sign your first paying clients and deliver massive results. However, we still want you to set an intention to increase your prices.

Knowing that you will increase your prices is motivating. It's also important that you make a commitment to do so when appropriate. Many coaches are too fearful to increase their rates, and stay at their starting price forever. We don't want you to fall into this trap.

Set an intention to increase your prices after your first X number of clients. We suggest you work with at least ten people before increasing your prices. After that many clients, you'll be in a great position to adjust your offer based on your experience, the feedback you've gained and the increase in your reputation.

Write your intention down so that you don't forget the commitment you made to yourself.

Action Steps

1. Follow the steps described in this chapter to define and price your first irresistible coaching offer.

2. Set an intention to increase your prices after your first ten paying clients.

3. Spend some time looking at your package and price, and say to yourself:

"My rate is _____."

Say it until you feel good about it. If you can't feel good about it, start over.

Action step three is critical. If you're not comfortable with your offer and pricing, you can't confidently market yourself. Practice saying your rates out loud until you feel confident.

———

Congratulations! You've defined your starting package and price. Let's go find you some paying clients. In the next chapter, you'll learn how to attract and sign paying clients as a new coach.

ATTRACTING CLIENTS WHEN STARTING OUT

So far in this book, you've researched your ideal clients and selected a coaching niche. You have also defined your first coaching offer. By now you may be wondering how on earth you go about finding potential clients.

Here's what you will learn in this chapter. First, we share the steps to sign your first paying client. Then we discuss five ways to find clients when starting out. One of the biggest problems you have as a new coach is that you have no following or email list. You don't yet have an eager audience of potential clients.

But that doesn't have to matter. The methods described in this chapter are designed to work whether you have a following of zero or thousands.

Steps to Sign Your First Client

Start by creating an outreach plan. This means selecting one or two ways to consistently reach out to potential clients. Later in this chapter, we share five outreach strategies that are ideal for new coaches. We ask you to pick one or two to try out for at least one month.

It's essential that you commit to doing outreach every day for *at least four weeks*. Yes, you're going to be scared. But that's okay. Fear is normal. Remember, fear is a sign that you're on the right track. If necessary, revisit Chapter Three for strategies to overcome self-doubt and take action anyway.

After executing your plan, evaluate your results. This step is critical. In fact, we recommend you evaluate as you go and not wait until the end of your first month. But let's say you perform consistent outreach for four weeks, and you have no clients. This might happen. It's NOT a reason to give up.

Here's what you should do instead. You review your results and refine your plan. Look at everything you did. Ask yourself why your outreach plan didn't work. Then improve your plan and keep going for another month.

Consistency is key here. You must keep doing outreach until you have perfected your offer and understand exactly what it is that your ideal client will pay for. The only way you will learn how to effectively market your services is through practice. You will fail. And this is okay. You are gathering data so that you can improve your process and try again.

Now let's look at the steps to attract clients in more detail.

Five Ways to Attract Clients

You are starting from scratch here. We're assuming you don't have an existing audience that you can share your offer with. If you do, fantastic! Go ahead and put your coaching offer out there to your email list or your social media followers.

But if you don't yet have a following, it's not a problem. Here are five methods you can use to find clients as a new coach…

1. Contact people you already know and tell them about your new coaching business.

2. Participate in forums and Facebook groups related to your topic. Answer questions and be a helpful and active member of the group.

3. Attend in-person networking groups and connect with people in real life. Look for ways you can give value and be of service to others in your local community.

4. Host a Meetup group around your coaching niche.

5. Create a Facebook group for people who would be your ideal clients.

The first method is to share with your personal network. Never underestimate the power of your personal network. These people already know you, trust you, and they want to support you. If they aren't a perfect fit for your coaching business, then they're willing to share your message with others who might be.

Don't be afraid to share your coaching offer with your personal network. You don't know who they might know. They might tell someone about you who winds up being your first client.

Of course, don't become the annoying network marketer who bombards her friends with sales posts. But there's nothing wrong with telling your connections about your new business. This can be as simple as sending emails to people you know and telling them about your offer. Or you can post announcements on your social media pages. Remember to ask people:

"Whom do you know who is struggling with problem X?", where X is the problem you help solve.

The second method is to participate in online groups. With this approach, you join a handful of forums or Facebook groups where your ideal clients hang out. Then show up each day and give value. Let people get to know and trust you. Become the go-to expert in your coaching topic. We recommend you make few or even no direct offers. Instead, be helpful and wait for people to come to you.

Tip: If you're interacting on social media, update your profiles to include a description of your coaching business and a link to your website. Make it easy for your ideal clients to get in touch with you.

The third method is to join local networking groups, for example, Business Network International (BNI) or your local Chambers of Commerce. This works well if you're good at connecting in person. Here are some tips to help you network with more confidence:

- Think of these events as a chance to build new relationships with your peers. This helps take the pressure off things. After all, it's fun to make new friends and be in the company of like-minded people.
- Practice starting conversations with other people. Be brave (it's not hard!) and keep it simple, for example, by saying: "Hi, we haven't met yet, what's your name?"
- Engage them in a conversation that focuses on them. Ask questions and don't talk about yourself yet. Be curious — if you can approach each new conversation from a place of genuine interest in the other person, then you will form much stronger connections.
- Wherever possible make appropriate referrals. Always think about how you can help others in the group. People will be eager to reciprocate without you needing to ask them.

Perhaps you love connecting in person, but there are no suitable networking groups in your area. That's okay —you can create your own! Method four is to start a local meetup group. Remember, when you connect in person, you create a sense of trust much faster than you can online. A local meetup group is a fast way to build genuine connections that can lead to new clients and referrals.

The final method to attract clients is through your own Facebook group. A Facebook group helps you connect with your audience, demonstrate your expertise and grow your business. However, it takes time to build a strong community. You must commit to giving people free value in your group before you start making offers. Here are a few things you can do to grow a Facebook group:

- Offer valuable content on a consistent basis.
- Give people a reason to join, such as a discount to coach with you or free training.
- Be present. Answer questions and interact with others.
- Ask fans to help you grow the group by sharing it with their network.
- Welcome people as they join the group.
- Stay on topic. Don't deviate.
- Ask relevant questions to encourage engagement.
- Create special content for your community, such as live Q&A videos or exclusive free training.

So how are you going to select which of these outreach strategies are best for you? Well, first, consider what resources you have. How large is your personal network? How much time do you have available to do outreach?

Also how do you best connect with people? Do you like to do this in person or online? Do you prefer groups? Or do you prefer one-on-one?

Perhaps you're extremely magnetic in person, but this doesn't come across in your writing or when you connect with others online. If so, take this into account. Play to your strengths.

And of course, always consider where your ideal clients are likely to be. Don't waste time attending a local business networking group if your audience is made-up of stay-at-home parents. You're unlikely to find clients — or even referrals to clients — in a business networking group.

Execute Your Outreach Plan

It's now time to execute your plan. We're going to warn you up front — you may not want to do this. You may start strong. But sooner or later, reaching out to people every day is going to become a challenge.

We recommend you set an outreach goal and then track your progress toward your goal. For example, you may commit to attending one networking event every week for the next four weeks. Or maybe you will post in three relevant Facebook groups every weekday for one month.

Next, set a time to do your outreach. Maybe you will attend a weekly networking event every Tuesday morning, host a weekly Meetup group every Wednesday afternoon, or connect with people on social media every weekday between 6 a.m. and 7 a.m. Put your outreach activity on your calendar as a recurring appointment. And make sure you show up when you said you would!

We also suggest you make a game of your outreach. View it as a fun experiment. Get curious about discovering what works for you. Enjoy the process and don't cling too tightly to the outcome.

Finally, track your outreach activities. For example, you might record what you did, whom you connected with and any outcomes in a spreadsheet. This will help keep you motivated and show you whether your strategy is working. It will also be an essential tool to help you follow up with people. Few contacts will become clients after the first meeting. Results come from consistent and genuine follow-up.

Evaluate Your Results

We want to be real with you here. It can take a lot of outreach to find your first paying client. You might be lucky, and you might connect with five people and sign your first client. But this isn't usually the case. It takes time to learn how to market your coaching services. And most of the people you connect with won't even be your ideal clients.

Don't let this put you off. Building any business is a gradual process. It starts slow. You might get zero results for the first few weeks. But then you begin to see some traction. People start reaching out to ask about your coaching services. Then you sign your first client. A week or two later, you sign your second client. You keep showing up and the momentum builds, until one day, you discover that you have a full coaching practice.

This is the result we want for you. A practice full of your ideal coaching clients. And to get there you must commit to consistent follow through and continuous improvement. Regardless of whether you have any paying clients, constantly evaluate your results.

When evaluating, you are looking to see what's working and what isn't working. Review your outreach strategy and your coaching package. Go back to your research notes on your ideal client. Are you connecting with the right people? Do you have an offer that's irresistible to them? Are you solving a burning pain? Are you communicating the value of your offer?

Take all this information and look for three ways you can improve your outreach strategy. This might mean tweaking your offer, adding a new marketing channel, changing the way you talk about your offer, adjusting your prices, etc.

Then keep executing your plan.

Action Steps

1. Review the five outreach methods and commit to doing one or two for the next month.

2. Put time on your calendar to make sure you consistently follow through with your outreach.

3. In your journal or a spreadsheet, start tracking the details of where and when you reach out to people.

4. At the end of every week and month, evaluate your results and look for three or more ways you can improve your strategy.

If you keep showing up and doing the work, people will start to inquire about working with you. So what do you do when that happens? That's the topic of the next chapter. You're about to learn how to conduct a discovery call that converts prospects into paying clients.

THE DISCOVERY CALL

You will never forget your first paying client as a coach. You'll remember where you were, what you were wearing and the feeling that rushed through your body when you made that first sale. It's a special moment. Signing your first client validates your decision to start your coaching business.

If you are selling a high-end service, the best way to make sales is to talk to your ideal clients on the phone or in a virtual meeting (for example, using Zoom). Before most people spend big bucks, they need more than a website to look at. They need that personalized touch, and they need to feel confident that you are the right coach to invest in. That means you must get proficient at making sales calls.

Just the phrase "sales call" makes a lot of people squirm. If you are anything like us, a vision of a sleazy used-car salesman trying to sell you an old jalopy pops into your head. We've all experienced the feeling of being pushed around and pressured into a sale. In this chapter we are going to turn that image around. How will you ever sign a client with that vision in your head?

We prefer to think of the initial conversation with a potential client as a discovery call. The purpose is not to sell someone on working with you. It's to find out whether you're a good fit for each other. And if it is, let the prospect know exactly how working with you will change their life.

In order to sign your first paying client, there are a few key components that you need to master.

The Right Mindset

Did you know that your mindset can prevent you from making a sale? It is true. Your mindset can keep you from making money through your coaching business. Your mindset can mean the difference between success and failure. If you are hung up on your own fears and insecurities, how do you expect anyone to pull out their credit cards and invest in you? You have to believe in yourself.

But more than that, you also have to let go of your attachment to making the sale. The moment you need to sign a client is the moment that you become pushy and convincing, even if you don't intend to.

The first thing you need to do is stop thinking of a sales call as something sleazy. Your role in these conversations is to help you and the potential client decide whether working together is a good fit. These calls are all about honesty and transparency. It isn't about you at all. It is about them. Stop being attached to the outcome. You will attract clients even if this specific phone call doesn't convert to a sale. This is not a call of desperation.

Do you believe in the transformation you provide to your clients? Are you comfortable with your price tag? If you have gone through the exercises in this book, the answers to both of these questions should be yes. And if your answers are yes, then your only job is to hold your potential clients as powerful people who can make up their own minds on whether the transformation is worth their time, effort and money.

Remember, they aren't investing in you. They are investing in their transformation through you. They aren't buying your services. They are buying their dreams and goals.

The Discovery Call Structure

Because each potential client is different, you don't want to follow a set script on your discovery calls. However, it's helpful to have a general structure and sequence. We'll give you some example questions to ask for each section of the call's framework, but it is critical that you ask questions that are authentic to you and reflect your own personal style.

Before every discovery call, take five minutes to disconnect and get your mind in the right place. Reaffirm to yourself the truth of your worth. Reconnect with your mission and message and to your ideal client. This process clears out any bad vibes and fears so that you can be completely present and serve your prospective client.

At the beginning of each call, set the tone for the conversation by creating a joint purpose and positioning yourself as the expert. It is important to establish the coach/client relationship from the beginning. It also relieves anxiety on both sides by letting the client know what to expect during your time together. By immediately putting the purpose of the call out in the open, neither side should be nervous when it comes time to "flip the switch" and talk about your program and the cost.

Remember, the purpose of the call is to see if working together is something that will benefit your client and if it is a good fit or not.

Put the purpose out there and make sure you are on the same page right away. For example, open by saying something like:

"Here is how I typically hold these calls. I'll ask you a lot of questions about your _____ to determine whether or not I can help you. If there is a way I can help you, I'll let you know. If it isn't a good fit, I'll let you know that, too, and try to point you in the right direction. Does that sound good to you?"

"Hi! I am excited about our conversation today. I understand you are interested in potentially working with me in one of my private coaching programs. Is that true?"

The next important part of the phone call is identifying the gap between where they are now and where they want to be… and why. Just as you worked to identify your big why, it is important to understand what motivates your potential client. Don't be afraid to dig deep. Keep asking why until you get to the bottom of the story.

Here are some sample questions to help you identify the gap:

"What makes you interested in working with a _____ coach?"

"What is it that made you invest the time on the phone today to fix _____?"

"Tell me more about _____."

"What else is going on?"

"So what do you want instead? What are you trying to gain specifically?"

The next portion of the call is to identify their challenges. Allow your client to become aware of what is not working in their lives. This isn't to be mean. This helps them realize where they need to change themselves before they can create new results. It may sound obvious, but a lot of people don't realize that something must give in order to arrive at the results they desire.

For example, you can ask your prospect:

"What is the biggest challenge you are facing right now?"

"What is the biggest obstacle for you to get to _____?"

"What have you tried so far to overcome _____?"

Next, determine how dedicated they are to change. Make sure your clients are committed and willing to do the work to make things happen. Change is not easy. Some questions you can ask are:

"How committed are you to _____?"

"Are you willing to do what it takes to change _____?"

"How much longer are you willing to continue as you are now?"

"On a scale of 1 to 10, how committed are you to changing?" "What would

make it a 10?"

By this point in the call, you and your potential client are clear on why this matters. You've built trust. Now it's time to ask if they are ready to work with you, but only if you're confident you can help them and want to work with them. Not everyone is a good fit for your coaching offer. And you should never pitch your coaching to someone who isn't your ideal client. This would be a disservice to both you and your prospect.

We recommend you ask permission before sharing your coaching offer. Often you won't even need to do that. If you follow the structure outlined above, many people will inquire about your coaching package without you needing to prompt them.

It is important to hold to your conviction during this part of the conversation. Don't let fear make you hesitate. Your client needs you to have strength and confidence.

If your prospective client doesn't inquire about working with you, here are some ways to present your offer:

"Would you like to hear more about what it would be like to work together?"

"Is it okay for me to explain a little bit about who I am as a coach and what it would look like if we worked together?"

"Based on our conversation, I recommend my _____ program. I recommend this program because _____. In our time together, we will (this is where you mirror back the key areas they want to change in their lives and how your program will help them do just that)."

Once the person says a resounding "YES," you now have your first paying client.

But you're not done yet! Be prepared on the phone call to facilitate payment. You can take payment over the phone or send a link to your payment system.

You can easily integrate PayPal and Stripe into your website or create a full-service checkout page with a system such as SamCart.

Also let your new client know what will come next. Build the excitement and let them know you care about them and the work they are about to start.

Handling Objections

You should never go into a discovery call with the mindset that you will need to handle objections, but it is good to have a plan to facilitate objections in a classy way should they come up.

Structure your call in a way that allows you to go into it with a mindset that you are committed to helping potential clients decide. This puts you at ease knowing that if you are meant to work together, you will. That being said, some people put up barriers to protect themselves. These barriers can come across as objections. Your role is to ask powerful questions about their objections to determine if they are stuck in a place of indecision or if they truly do not feel that it is a good fit.

Let's explore some of the most common objections and how to handle them.

Objection: "I Can't Afford It"

Money is a touchy topic. When someone says they can't afford your program, it may or may not be the truth. You should be tactful and compassionate as you dig for the answer, for example, by asking:

"I hear that you don't believe you can afford it. Is it okay for me to ask you a question about that?"

"If you did have the money, is this something that you would want to pursue?"

"What would you need to get out of the program to make it worth it for you?"

"How can we make this happen for you?"

If, during the call, your potential client demonstrates how urgent and important their problem is, they may be open to finding a way to pay for your program. Offer to help. If you have a payment plan, bring it up.

Objection: "I Have to Think About It"

If your potential client says, "I have to think about it," it may be that they want to politely excuse themselves from the call. Or it may mean they still have questions. Or perhaps they aren't ready to commit. However, if you end the call without finding the truth, then you are allowing this person to crawl back into their own doubts and fears. Instead, inquire further. For example, by asking one of the following questions.

"What do you need to know in order to make a decision?"

"Are there other questions I can help answer that I haven't covered already?"

"What specifically do you need to think about?"

If your potential client has to think about his or her decision, there is typically an underlying concern. It could be money, or it could be something else. Get to the bottom of it so that you can empower your potential client to decide. Hold them accountable, just as you will if they choose to join your program.

Objection: "I Have to Ask My Spouse"

This objection may not be an objection at all. It's generally a good idea to make big decisions with your spouse. However, this objection could be rooted in something else. They may be using this as an excuse because they have a fear of investing in themselves or making a commitment to change. Again, dig a little deeper.

"Great! Is there something specific you need to speak with him/her about?"

"I understand that. So are you saying you are in if your spouse agrees? Or is there something else?"

"Can I jump on the phone with you and your spouse tomorrow to answer any questions?"

If you discover the issue is really the money involved, ask more questions about that. If you find out they have other concerns, address them. If they want to talk to their spouse, set up a follow-up phone call to address any new issues.

Here is a painful truth. If you embrace this truth, you will grow into a better coach. When a client has an objection, it typically means they haven't seen the value of what you are offering. Even if they claim they do, subconsciously they don't. If you are getting a lot of objections, it may be time to check in with yourself. You've heard of the law of attraction, right? Your potential clients might be holding up a mirror for you. For example, if you've been unwilling to invest in yourself because you "can't afford it," you might be attracting people in that same mindset. Or if you don't have confidence in yourself, your clients may not have confidence in you, either.

Signing Your First Client

We have laid out the entire framework for your business. At this point, you may be wondering when you might expect to land your first paying customer.

Well, it depends. But the good news is that if you take the necessary steps to set your business up correctly, it shouldn't take you long.

We surveyed several coaches and asked them how long it took to find their first paying client. The answers ranged from immediately to four months. Their clients came from all the way to paid advertising. Those coaches who took the time to build an authentic business were able to get paying clients quicker. Let's look at a few case studies.

In Melissa's case, her blog (which she wrote to inspire working mothers) naturally progressed into a coaching program after several readers inquired if she would coach them through specific issues. Because Melissa already had an email list of nearly 1,000 loyal blog readers, her first client found her before she launched the coaching side of her business. However, after she was up and running as an official coach, she signed another client just three days later.

Melissa's first month coaching led to an income of just over $1,000. That was with two clients in the one-on-one coaching model. Three months later, Melissa had signed an additional three clients and made $3,500 that month. All of her initial clients came through her blog and referrals.

As she shared in the introduction, Sally signed three coaching clients after sending just one email to her small (fewer than 1,000) email list. Sally then continued to attract new clients through her blog, published books and private Facebook group.

Another business coach we surveyed found her first client three months after starting her business. She grew her business slowly as a side hustle while she maintained her full-time job. She built an email list and a private Facebook group. She coached several people for free to hone her skills and get testimonials. Once she felt ready, she pitched her services to her Facebook group and immediately had two clients sign on. She now has a subscription-based coaching service for her business and is aiming to leave her nine-to-five job.

There is no one right path to attract your first clients. The key is to do what feels natural to you. Play to your strengths and trust that you can help people. Keep showing up and making offers. Do this and you will start signing your first clients.

Action Steps

1. Write out the framework for your discovery calls along with questions that are authentic to your voice, your message and your business. Walk through your discovery call out loud.

2. Determine the probing questions you will ask if objections arise. Again, make sure your questions are authentic and feel good to you.

3. Decide how you will celebrate your first paying customer.

———

Up next, we discuss what to do during your paid client calls that you can show up and confidently coach your clients to create amazing results in their lives.

10

WINNING COACHING CALLS

This chapter was contributed by a coaching friend, Pauline Cheung, and edited by the authors.

L et's start by getting clear about the purpose of a coaching conversation. What do you do as a coach? How exactly do you serve your clients?

The main objective of a coaching conversation is to help your client get clarity or insight on a topic related to their goals. You help them get more out of themselves so that they can achieve their goal faster than they would by themselves. You also help clients become the person they need to be to take the required action to get where they want to go.

Note: The first and last coaching sessions differ from a general coaching session. We'll cover more on these sessions later in this chapter.

Once the client has gained new insight, the coaching conversation usually concludes with your client taking ownership and accountability on what action they will take. That action could be an actual task (or series of tasks) they will complete. Or it might be a new ongoing practice that will help them embody the traits of the person they want to become.

Sometimes, what stops people from acting is not knowing how to do something or what to do. Other times, it's their current mindset that holds them back. The work of a coach is in helping a client shift the way they see themself into a version that creates results.

Consulting vs. Therapy vs. Coaching

While we're defining things, it's also helpful to understand the differences between coaching, consulting and therapy. Now as a coach, this doesn't mean you can't bring in some element of consulting (for example) into the work you do with your clients. But it is helpful to recognize when you are doing this.

A consultant provides expertise to solve a problem. They'll first understand the problem and then provide a solution or a set of recommendations for the client to implement. The confusion between coaching and consulting is understandable as many business coaches offer a useful blend of coaching and consulting. It is quite acceptable to take this approach in your coaching practice. The key is to be aware of when you're wearing a "consulting hat" versus a "coaching hat."

In therapy, the therapist is the expert in addressing psychological issues. They make a specific diagnosis and help the patient heal from it and become fully functional again. Therapy is focused on fixing and healing. A coach's role isn't to diagnose or heal a past trauma; it's focused on helping the client move forward. The confusion with therapy is most likely because coaching can bring in emotions too.

Finally, coaching is more of a partnership than a hierarchical expert-client process. It's focused on creation, helping a client move forward to create something new they desire. The International Coach Federation (ICF) defines coaching as "partnering with clients in a thought-provoking and creative process that inspires them to maximize their personal and professional potential."

A coach does not need to be an expert in the client's work, although some understanding can make the coaching easier. In consulting, the consultant provides the answers, whereas in coaching, the client comes up with their own answers.

Styles of Coaching

There isn't one specific style of coaching, and with experience you will find your own style. Knowing your coaching style helps you attract your ideal client. Different clients need different coaches to help them move forward, so there's space for all coaches to do well.

To find your style, start by asking yourself these questions:

What big-name coaches do you resonate with?

How would you describe their style?

For example, consider the styles of Tony Robbins (high energy) versus Martha Beck (spiritual) versus Marshall Goldsmith (corporate).

If it's hard to identify specific coaches, think about the personal development books that resonate most with you.

What do you like about their style that works for you?

How would you describe the way they delivered their message?

Take your time to experiment with different styles to find what feels natural for you. It's also good to develop your "range," as some clients will want more pushing than others.

Asking Questions for Results

An important part of coaching is asking the right kind of questions to help your client find clarity or insight. With coaching, you help your client open up and explore themselves in order to reveal fresh insight. Hence, open questions are more powerful than closed questions. Let's look at the difference between the two.

Closed questions can be answered with a yes or no and are generally not good for inviting further exploration. Although, occasional use is okay, for example, to confirm something or to check in with your client.

Here's an example of a closed question: "I'd like to check in with you. Is X really the issue?"

If your client says yes, then great, you can continue coaching on it. If they say no, you could then follow up with: "What is the real issue then?" Or if they seem uncertain, then that would be rich grounds to further probe and coach around.

In most of your coaching, ask open questions. Open questions typically begin with "What" or "How." Effective open questions are concise and focused on the client, not the problem.

An open question can also start with "Why." However, be cautious when using a "Why" question. For some clients, these types of questions can trigger some defensiveness or a natural tendency to justify a current position or belief that is not serving them.

Here are some examples of open questions:

What would you like to get out of this session?

What is most important about this for you?

What would be most exciting for you?

How does this relate to your life purpose?

What would you do if you were not afraid?

It's a year from now and you overcame X (or achieved Y). What does life look like for you?

What would a 10 out of 10 look like in this area of your life?

What is this really about? (e.g. When a client describes a situation, the problem isn't always the real issue, it's the client's thoughts about their circumstances.)

Who do you need to be in order to achieve X?

What are you avoiding?

What do you get by holding onto Y? (Y is the thing they say they want to get rid of, e.g. procrastination.)

What will happen if you do and what will happen if you don't?

What would you do if you trusted yourself?

What would help you decide?

Where do you give your power away? To whom?

How are you sabotaging yourself?

What's the story you're telling yourself?

If you were honoring your values, what would this look like?

What else?

What are your takeaways from this session?

What action will you commit to?

General Structure of a Coaching Session

Now that we've covered the basics, let's dissect the structure of a typical coaching session. This will help you stay focused and have productive coaching calls.

After a quick opening to establish rapport, most of the conversation is spent asking questions to explore the client's thinking and to find a path forward. The session usually ends with laying out some action steps to take.

Here's a general structure you can follow in your coaching sessions:

1-2-Minute Icebreaker

Spend the first couple of minutes reconnecting with your client, and have them get present in the session. You may ask the client to focus on a few breaths to help them become centered and present in the coaching session.

Homework/Successes Recap

Follow up from the previous coaching session, and see what new learnings the client has realized for themselves during the interval between sessions. Acknowledge and celebrate any new successes the client has had. Also note down any major issues that may have also crept up.

Topic for the Session

Having a topic and also asking the client what it is that they want to get from the topic are important. This gives the session a focus so that the client can get some clarity and come up with actions to take. Coaching is mainly about forward movement. Without a focus for the session, you can spend too much time with the client rehashing a story and not making progress.

Exploration

Most of the coaching session will be spent helping the client in the following ways:

- Getting clarity around the topic you and your client have chosen.

- Exploring their current versus desired state.
- Uncovering what the mindset block is, if any. Help reflect to your client what they're not seeing without making them wrong. Address what's getting in the way. How would they like to be instead? Whom would they have to be?
- Helping them see new insight or realize something new in themselves.
- Showing a client how they are limiting themselves, for example, by holding onto a past story. Sometimes, you may need a bolder (but still compassionate) approach to do this.
- Providing advice/recommendations/strategies if the topic is around a skill or knowledge gap that the client has and you can fulfill. As we discussed above, this falls into the realm of consulting. So acknowledge you're providing consulting rather than coaching when the need arises.

Options and Next Steps

Help your client identify what new options are available to them and what they will choose for themselves.

Commitment to Action and Accountability

The session typically ends with some type of action item that will help the client move forward on the area of focus. This could be choosing one of the options identified in the session and acting on it. Other times, the action item will be an exercise, e.g. journaling, to help the client get further clarity on what was uncovered during the session. The key is to have some accountability on what they will do after the call and by when. There's something about announcing an action out loud that helps to reinforce this commitment.

After the Session

It's not your job to judge your client, whether they complete the action or not. If they do, then celebrate and check for what they learned from taking this action. If they didn't, get curious.

Maybe they came up with a more suitable action. Perhaps an emergency prevented them from following through, or maybe they realized after the coaching session that something else was what they really wanted.

Often, you will notice that your client procrastinates or makes excuses for themself. All humans have recurring behavior patterns that limit their results. When this happens, you have a new opportunity to coach your client and help them achieve their goals.

Most of the work/transformation happens between calls. So don't get attached to the client having to take action or experience an epiphany during a conversation. Trust that your clients are resourceful and in charge of their lives.

Also do not see their failure to complete something as a failure on your part. Provided you're showing up for your client, giving them your complete attention and helping them see how their thoughts and emotions are creating their results, then you are doing your job as a coach. The rest is up to the client.

First Paid Session With a Client

The first and last paid sessions with a client differ in the general structure.

After someone signs on to become an ongoing client, the first session lays the groundwork for your future sessions together. Quite often, the client may never have had any prior coaching, and even if they have, their previous coach might have had a different style or approach than you.

The focus of the first session is to create a foundation of trust and openness between yourself and the client in order to build a successful coaching relationship with one another. This allows the client to bring their full self into the coaching and get the most out of it. Coaching is an intensely personal and vulnerable experience, so establishing trust with your client is paramount.

The following is a suggested list of agenda items to cover in the first paid session. It's not necessary to do everything. Pick and choose what would be applicable for you and your client.

Confidentiality and Trust

Reassure the client and help them bring their full self into the coaching. Ask the client what they would need in order to feel they were in a trusting and judgement-free zone. A client will not open up if they feel judged.

Clarify Goals

Explore the overall goals your client wants from your coaching. For example, you can ask one of these questions:

- Where do you want to be in a year's time?
- Where do you want to be at the end of our coaching engagement?

Visioning

Conduct a visioning exercise to help your client picture what their life will be like when they have achieved their goals. If the client starts to lose their way several weeks in, this vision is something you can use to help them reset. Some questions you can ask are:

- What does life look like when you've reached your goal?
- What do you see? What is your environment like?
- How do you show up differently?
- How do you think and feel differently?
- What does a typical day look like?

Identify Values

Help clients get clear on what their values are. Identify which values are tied to the goal they're seeking help with. Knowing which values are underpinning a client's goal helps them stick with it, especially when the work gets hard or uncomfortable.

Another way to look at it is to know the 'why' that's driving your client's goals. You could provide a worksheet to the client to complete beforehand and bring along to the session.

Obstacles

Explore what obstacles or gaps might get in the way of their success. Focus on the ones that they're in control of, for example, mindset, lack of training or knowledge, or lack of support system. These can become topics to work through in future coaching sessions.

Accountability

Find out how the client likes to be held accountable. Some clients may need more of a "tough-love" approach to get them to stay accountable to their actions. Others might prefer gentler reminders.

What Else?

Do you or your client have other expectations from the coaching relationship? It's good to have this addressed in the beginning. For example, you might let new clients know that when you interrupt them, you're not trying to be rude. You're being in service of them, especially when time is limited, and you'd like them to home in on what's important about the story they're telling you.

.

Last Paid Session With a Client

The last session of your engagement with a client is typically referred to as a completion session. This is where you help your client take stock of everything they've achieved during your time together. It's also a time to help them celebrate and identify what's next for them.

During this session you can do the following:

Acknowledge and Celebrate

Take your client back to the beginning of the coaching relationship and emphasize the changes, progress or milestones they've achieved through working together. Celebrate and acknowledge your client.

Recap Learnings

Have the client highlight what learnings have been most important and transformational for them.

Anchoring

Explore how they want to anchor these learnings and how they plan to practice or embody them going forward. For example, they may do this in the form of daily affirmations or a meditation. Maybe they have a symbolic object that they will carry or display prominently. Or perhaps they will practice an exercise when they become aware of themselves slipping back into a negative habit.

What's Next?

Explore what's next for them in terms of growth. How do they plan to continue making progress in the topic you've coached them on? Often, a client will sign up for another coaching package with you.

Feedback and Testimonial

Check if they have any feedback for you and/or request a testimonial from them.

Action Steps

1. Start thinking about your specific style of coaching.

2. Plan out a structure for your coaching conversations.

You now have everything you need to start your coaching business and sign your first clients. In the final chapters, we cover more advanced topics so that you can grow your new business. Coming up next, you'll learn how to develop your online practice and start attracting more of your ideal clients.

11

YOUR ONLINE PRESENCE

Okay, it is time to put yourself out there in a bigger way. Saying that may make you feel uncomfortable, but as a coach, you need to become accustomed to being present online.

Technically, you don't need to take this step to start coaching. You can and should sign your first few clients using the outreach strategies discussed in Chapter Eight. This will help you confirm whether coaching is the right career path for you before you invest in a website and other marketing strategies.

But eventually, you will want to scale your business. And to do that in today's digital world, you need an online presence. Think about it. Have you shelled out a bunch of money to someone you didn't look up online? Before choosing a new coach, most prospects will first read your blog, follow you on social media, watch your videos, read your emails, etc.

In this chapter we cover the basics for putting yourself out there and developing your online presence.

Naming Your Coaching Practice

If you haven't already done so, pick a name for your coaching practice. Every business needs a name. It gives credibility and allows you to brand yourself. While you can rename your business down the road, there are some headaches associated with doing so.

Naming your business is an important step. Spend some time and don't rush yourself here. There are three main considerations to take into account when you choose a name for your coaching practice.

#1: Name for Branding

Branding is so important for your coaching business because it helps set you apart from the sea of other coaches competing online. When you select your business name, keep branding in mind. Some coaches choose to use their own personal name for their business, which is perfectly acceptable. Others choose to name their business with a catchy phrase or words that portray a vision. With either option, keep in mind that your practice's name should be easy to remember and easy to spell. You should also think about the associated social media handles.

For example, if your name is Melissa Stocksocovtys (totally made that up by randomly typing letters on the keyboard), that may be a tough name to brand. People aren't going to be able to say it, spell it or remember it.

If you choose a catchy business name, make sure you use straightforward spelling of all words. Some people get caught up in being clever but later regret it. For example, they may purposely misspell a word or use an alternate spelling to be cute, but clients can't remember how to spell the name of their businesses later. Always choose "irresistible" over "ear-resistible" no matter how appealing you find the latter.

Also check whether anyone else is using the same name. There are a few ways you can do this. If you're filing a DBA (which is short for "doing business as" and indicates an informal business name) you can check with your local county clerk's office. Or, if you're filing the name of your corporation or limited liability company, you can check with your state's Secretary of State, which approves business entity filings. Finally, search to see if a similar name is trademarked. You can use the U.S. Patent and Trademark Office's trademark search tool to do this.

#2: Name for Niche

You spent a lot of time carefully choosing your niche, and you want your clients to know what you do the second they land on your website or see your business card. There are a few different ways to accomplish this, and one of them is through naming.

For example, if you name your business "Coaching with Sarah," your clients may be confused. What type of coaching do you do? Whom do you coach? They won't be able to tell, and they may move on without spending the time to figure it out. However, if you add in words that help differentiate you, you can alleviate that confusion.

For example, you could expand your name to: "Relationship Coaching with Sarah" or "Sarah: Executive Performance Coach." But you don't have to use your name. You can simply name your business for your niche.

One successful example of naming for niche is Steve Kamb. His business is called Nerd Fitness and he helps "nerds, misfits, and mutants lose weight, get strong, and get healthy." Yes, we took those words straight from his website. As of 2020, he has a team of 25 full-time coaches and a massive global community. Steve's distinctive branding is a significant component of his success.

#3: Name for Transition

You may not be thinking about the future of your business just yet, but someday you may choose to expand or sell your practice. Some business names make this much easier to accomplish. For example, if you later choose to bring another coach into your practice, you may have to rename and rebrand if you're using your own name as your business. The same applies if you sell your business.

You work hard to build up your brand and name recognition. And you may lose a lot of that hard work if you rename down the road.

Again, these are all only considerations. Feel free to name your business anything you like! Naming is a fun step in the process of setting up your coaching business.

Tagline

In addition to your business name, you need a tagline to go along with it. A tagline is a short phrase that quickly lets people know what your business is about. When someone lands on your site for the first time, you have about three seconds to grab their attention. You do this through the appearance of your website, your business name and your tagline.

You can choose to write a catchy slogan or perhaps simply a few words describing exactly what you do. Either way, you want the people who arrive on your site to know within three seconds what you and your business are all about.

Taglines can benefit you by:

- Differentiating you from other coaches in the same industry
- Defining the coaching experience you offer
- Painting a picture of you and your unique personality
- Telling potential clients what to expect when working with you

Your tagline can evolve as you evolve, so don't worry about getting it right the first time. Here are some questions to ask yourself as you develop your tagline.

- What is your business all about (in 7 to 10 words)?
- What problems do you help your clients solve?
- What solutions do you offer your clients?
- What keywords stand out to you when you think about your business?
- Can you put those keywords together into one phrase?

Brainstorm several different taglines. See which one feels like a good fit for you.

Here are some examples we came up with to get your creative juices flowing:

Wellness Coach: Improving Digestion One Belly at a Time

Leadership Coaching: Inspiring Executives to Lead the Right Way

Business Coach: Set Your Business Apart

You can keep it simple, too. A formula you can use is "I help _____ with _____." Many times, clear trumps clever.

Building Your Website

Now it's time for the techy stuff. Like we mentioned before, you don't absolutely need a website to coach. However, at some point in time if you are looking to grow, you may wish you had started a website earlier.

Websites give your potential clients a place to look around and get to know you without feeling any pressure. They get to put a face with a name. They get a feeling of what it's like to work with you. A website also allows you to start collecting names and email addresses to build your email list.

If you're not familiar with building an email list, don't worry. We talk more about this in Chapter Fourteen. The goal of your email list is to build a connection with people over time. As you develop a relationship with people on your email list, some will eventually become clients.

Luckily, building a website doesn't have to be expensive or complicated.

In order to start your website, you need the following pieces:

1. Domain Name — This is your website address. It can be the name of your coaching business (if available). You can search for available names on Bluehost or Go Daddy.

2. Hosting Provider — This is the company that stores your website on their server. There are several available. FastComet and Bluehost are good options for someone starting out. There are some free options available, but skip the urge to use these. Website hosting is not expensive, and it will give you a professional look.

3. Website Content Management System — This is the framework that makes up your website. We use and recommend WordPress.org. You can start out using one of the many free themes. Then upgrade to a more advanced theme when you are ready.

You can pay someone to set all of this up for you, or you can spend a day and figure it out on your own. If you decide to do the latter, Sally has a step-by-step guide on how to set up a website here: sallyannmiller.com/buildwebsite

Once you get your website up and running, you'll need a few pages.

1. Home Page – This is the page your visitors first land on, so it's one of the most important pages on your website. You want to convince visitors to stick around and learn more about you and your services. Make your home page unique and welcoming. You want your potential clients to feel the magic right away. Convey how working with you will make them feel and why they should hire you. You can do this by using pictures of you, testimonials, and a confident color palette. Help them paint the picture of their upcoming transformation.

2. About Page – This is the page where you can let your light shine. Your About page is about you and your clients. Tell your story. Show a little vulnerability by demonstrating your unique life experiences, and then position yourself as an expert by showing them how you overcame the obstacles. Also talk about who your clients are. Explain what they get from working with you. Your About page is one of the most read pages on your website, so don't waste this opportunity to sell the transformation you deliver. Get creative!

3. Services Page – This is a page highlighting the services you offer. It serves as your sales page. This page is where your messaging comes together to sell the transformation you offer. You need to dive deep into your ideal client's world and use wording that conveys you not only understand where they are stuck and why, but that you can help them overcome the challenges they are facing. We'll cover more on this later. There is much debate on whether you should list your pricing on your website. There's no right or wrong choice. Ultimately, it comes down to whatever feels right to you.

4. Checkout Page – If you offer group programs, you need the ability to handle payments on your website. You can use PayPal or Stripe for accepting credit card payments. If you only work with one-on-one clients, you can skip this step and simply send new clients an invoice direct from PayPal.

5. Contact Page – This is a page letting potential clients know how to get in touch with you.

6. Blog – This is an optional section of your website. You do not have to have a blog, although it can be a good way to build trust and loyal subscribers

that may eventually turn into clients. We'll talk more about the role of blogging and other online content in Chapter Thirteen.

Social Media

Social media is an established way to connect with other coaches and potential clients. It can also help you spread your message to a far-reaching audience. You can build a tribe of loyal followers and potential clients through social media sites such as Facebook, Twitter, LinkedIn, Instagram, and Pinterest. We probably left a few out of that list. However, don't attempt to manage them all.

Social media can suck hours out of your day if you let it. And just when you feel as though you have a handle on it, the latest trend changes everything. Our advice is to pick one or two social media platforms to focus on. Choose the ones where the people in your niche are most likely to be found and keep a consistent presence there.

If you try to balance every social media platform by yourself, one of two things will inevitably happen:

1. You will spend a lot of valuable time on social media, and these are not paid hours.

2. Some of your social media platforms will end up neglected, and you will come across as unprofessional when people go to follow you only to find that you haven't been active for months.

As you start to scale your business, you may choose to hire a social media virtual assistant who can keep your profiles up to date and ensure comments are answered in a timely manner. Until then, automate where you can to save time. You can use a tool like Buffer to schedule future posts. There are many other automation tools out there, so research and find the ones that fit your needs.

Before we get to the action steps, we have some words of support for you. If you found this chapter overwhelming, we urge you to take it one step at a time. Focus on one task from start to completion before tackling the next. Build your brand online intentionally and thoughtfully. Don't feel like you have to rush through it. You can do this!

Action Steps

1. Choose the name of your business by evaluating naming for branding, niche and transition. Brainstorm ideas until you find one that feels amazing to you.

2. Develop your tagline by answering the questions outlined in this chapter. Don't fret if you don't get it right the first time. Taglines are easy to change. Tweak it until you fall in love with it.

3. Build your website. This action step is going to take some time, and that's okay. Your website is an important part of your business. But once again, it doesn't have to be perfect right away. Websites are easy to change as often as you need to, and they tend to evolve right along with you and your business. Consider outsourcing the techy side so that you can focus on the content. Get the basics together and start putting yourself out there online.

4. Determine which social media platforms (no more than three) you will focus on in the beginning. Research where your target audience is hanging out. Set up your profiles with similar branding to your website (same pictures, wording and feel). Commit to how often you will update each platform and then stick to it. Consistency is much more important than quantity. If you can't update daily, that is fine. Choose a frequency that works for you. Consider automation tools to save you time and energy.

––––––––––

When you're ready, proceed to the next chapter, where you'll learn how to cover yourself legally in your new business.

12

THE LEGAL STUFF

Early on in your practice, there is one thing you absolutely must do. You must cover yourself legally. This isn't most people's favorite topic but it is a necessary step for a new coach. So we'll keep it short and sweet. And don't worry, this doesn't have to be complex.

When we first started out, we both skipped this step. Looking back, we're fortunate that nothing came from that decision. However, we have spoken with a fellow coach who was not so fortunate. She was sued by a client and ended up losing a lot of money because she failed to take a few legal steps. Don't fall into that trap.

Neither of us is a lawyer by any means, so please do your own research and speak to an attorney to make decisions that best suit you and your business.

Business Considerations

Depending on where you live, you'll probably have to establish yourself with the government so that you can pay taxes on your earnings and write off business expenses. There are a couple of common ways to do this.

Most coaches start out as either a sole proprietor or a limited liability company.

Becoming a sole proprietor is the easiest, fastest and cheapest way to start running your business. Coaches often choose this option when they are first starting out, and that is totally acceptable, especially until you validate that becoming a life coach is what you really want. Setting up your business as a sole proprietor is simple, but the downside is that you have no liability protection. If someone sues you and wins, they could have access to your assets, including your personal assets not related to your business.

A limited liability company (LLC) has the benefit of liability protection. If someone were to sue you and win, that person would generally be limited to the assets of the LLC. He or she would not be able to access your personal assets such as your car or home. The downside to an LLC is that you have to pay fees and fill out paperwork to file.

We both started out as sole proprietors. Then once we became more established, we started the paperwork to file for an LLC. This worked out well for us. Pick the path that suits you and your personal situation.

Legal Forms and Waivers

Coaching is not therapy or medical treatment, but your clients may not be aware of this fact. You do not diagnose or treat people medically. It is in your best interest to provide a written disclosure to ensure your clients are on the same page as you.

Also lay out an agreement of your services based on the coaching package your client has chosen. Be specific on payment terms, refund policies, and what happens if your client is late or misses an appointment. This will alleviate any headaches you may experience down the line when one of your clients misses payment or misses an appointment.

Website Terms and Conditions

Yes, your website needs some legal jargon as well. You'll spend a lot of time and energy creating the content on your site, and you want to protect it. Your website terms and conditions do not have to be complex, but you should approach the project with the goal of having them hold up in court.

Your terms and conditions are unique to your business and what you offer, but you should provide a few of the basics.

- Limit Liability — Your website may contain errors every now and again, so you'll want a statement protecting you from any errors in the content provided. If you allow comments from your readers, add in a blurb that limits you from liability from anything offensive someone might post.
- Copyright — Include a notice about copyright to protect your content.
- Privacy Policy — You are likely going to collect information from people who visit your website to add to your email list. If you do, you'll need a privacy policy statement to let people know how you use that information.

In some cases, you may enlist the help of an attorney, but a simple Google search of "terms and conditions generator" gives you a lot of options to get started with (and many of them are free). You can also browse other coaching websites to get an idea of what you may need, but do not blatantly copy anyone else's terms.

Most coach/client relationships don't end in legal hassles, but there is always a potential. Misunderstandings happen, and you can protect yourself by having an agreement in writing signed by both parties. Eliminate as much confusion as possible and protect yourself.

Action Steps

1. Decide which legal entity you would like to pursue for your business and file the appropriate paperwork.

2. Add your legal terms to your website.

3. Write your liability waiver.

In the next chapter, you'll learn how to position yourself as an expert in your niche so that you can quickly attract more of your ideal clients.

13

POSITIONING YOURSELF AS AN EXPERT

When potential clients discover your business, you must immediately come across as an expert in your field. In their eyes, you want to be the obvious choice as their coach. You have the knowledge and experience to help people change their lives. It is your job to convey that message to your audience. In order to inspire confidence and attract clients that pay a premium for your services, you must consistently and persistently position yourself as an expert.

A common fear that you may experience is that you're not good enough. We don't want you to let fear stop you from starting your amazing career as a coach. If you feel self-doubt creep in, follow these tips to move past it.

1. Nip negative thoughts in the bud. Self-doubt and fear are real, and they are part of every journey that you choose to undertake. When those inner doubts start to bubble up in your mind, recognize them for what they are. Don't let them fester or continue to grow. Disrupt the thought pattern before it takes over.

2. Recognize past accomplishments. Think of times in your past when you have overcome fear and done something amazing. You did it then, and you can do it again. In fact, some of the biggest accomplishments in our lives are the ones we had to overcome fear to achieve. Self-doubts and fear are most often just monsters in our mind that attempt to keep us within our comfort zones.

3. Don't go it alone. If you are feeling fear and uncertainty, talk it through

with someone close to you. Chances are, once you start speaking your fear out loud, you will see that your thoughts had become distorted and exaggerated in your mind. Also join an online community with people who are in a similar position to you. Sometimes our friends and family don't understand the challenges of starting a new business. You can join Sally's online community (it's free!) by visiting the bonus area here: sallyannmiller.com/coachbook.

4. Keep a journal. Journaling is a useful habit in many ways. One of the benefits of journaling is that it will help you process and deal with self-doubt and fear. You gain clarity once you have your issue laid out on paper. You can detail your fears and find solutions. A journal also allows you to look back at the positive things in your life. We are often quick to forget our successes and all the obstacles we've overcome because our brains automatically focus on the negative. Journaling helps break this habit, as it offers a realistic perspective and record of your life.

The truth is that you are an expert in your niche. You have something to offer your clients, and we don't want fear to keep you from serving those you are called to serve.

Positioning yourself as an expert will not only give your clients confidence in you, but it will also give you added belief in yourself. Let's dive in and find out how you can position yourself as an expert.

Should You Get Certified as a Coach?

This topic is debatable. There are successful coaches who hold certifications, and successful coaches who do not. We're not going to give you a definitive answer here, but you can decide for yourself what is best for you and your business.

There are advantages to being certified. Certifications give you instant credibility. They are like college degrees. They prove that you have had training from a professional.

Coaching is a skill that may or may not come naturally to you, but it can be learned. You have the knowledge and experience you need to be an expert in your field, but do you know how to help clients reach their full potential? Do you know how to guide them instead of advise them? Do you know how to ask powerful questions and help clients dig deep within themselves? A good coaching certification program teaches you these skills.

Certification can also set you apart from other coaches who are uncertified. It shows that you care enough about your business to invest in yourself and be the best you can be. Because coaching is an unregulated field, it is full of coaches who are looking to make a quick buck without investing in themselves.

Finally, investing in yourself and getting certified increases the chances that you stick with your coaching business even if things get rough.

However, certification can be expensive. A good program starts in the low four figures. Sally was certified with The Life Coach School and paid $18,000. The training and knowledge gained through this yearlong experience were invaluable. However, you need to be certain that you want to be a life coach before making such a large investment.

If you are a new coach looking to succeed, consider investing in a coaching certification program, but only after you've stepped your toe in the waters and are confident that this is the path for you. There are many to choose from at many different price points. The decision is ultimately yours to make.

Professional Appearance

Coaches have a unique career. We are here to serve our clients, and we must put our clients above all else. This means that no matter how we feel on a personal level, we must pull ourselves together and focus on our clients. It means that we must be professional at all costs. A single unprofessional tweet or client call can cost you and your business big time. Spelling and grammar errors can cause your clients to go with another option.

It is up to us as coaches to put our best foot forward all the time. From a professional website to a professional physical appearance, all are important.

Don't get caught looking unprofessional by accident. If you have a scheduled Skype or Zoom call, make sure you're dressed to impress, even if this is an audio-only call. You never know when someone might ask you to switch to video.

It is our responsibility to serve our clients by being our best, most professional self. That means that every tweet, every podcast and every client call must be delivered as the professional coach we intend to be. By maintaining ourself professionally, we immediately position ourself as an expert that our clients look up to.

Create Amazing Content

The content that we post speaks as much as the words that come out of our mouths. As a coach, you want to post a lot of valuable content to attract your clients. In fact, in our experience, it has been our content that has attracted most of our clients. People are pulled in and interested in working with us because they identify with what we write about. Your content can be comprised of many things.

Blog Posts

Sharing blog posts and other forms of content marketing builds your credibility and provides valuable and free content to your audience of future clients. Often, people need to see your message several times before making the decision to invest in you. They need to feel a real connection with you, and blogging provides this connection.

Write about topics that are directly related to your area of expertise and the struggles your clients are facing. Don't hold back when it comes to giving solutions and practical strategies your clients can implement. Your clients aren't paying for what you know. There is so much free information available on the internet. They are paying for the personalized and customized approach and accountability that you offer. Not all coaches maintain a blog, but it can be an amazing way to bring in clients and widen your reach.

Email Newsletters

As you start to build your tribe, keep them engaged by providing additional content not available on your blog. You can do this through weekly or biweekly emails.

These emails keep your name fresh on their minds because your readers may not visit your blog or website on a weekly basis. Email newsletters also give you the opportunity to sell to a highly primed market. You can offer exclusive discounts and opportunities not available to the general public.

Social Media

Many of your followers know you by what you tweet, pin or post. Offer valuable tips and quick bits of inspiration related to your business. Link back to your blog and website pages. Share live videos. Encourage interaction. The goal is that your followers recognize you and your message, your voice, and business name, because they see these often and associate them with great content.

Free Incentives

Another piece of content you can offer is a free opt-in incentive. This can be an eBook, checklist, video series, or any other piece of content that you trade for email addresses. Think about your ideal audience and what they are struggling with. How can you add value and help them with a problem? We will discuss your email list more in the next chapter.

Gather Testimonials

Testimonials are a must for coaches. Because coaching is all about the results and transformation, people want to hear about other people's positive experiences in your programs. They want to have an extra layer of comfort knowing that it is possible for them, too. Testimonials build trust and ease some of your potential clients' fear and resistance.

You may wonder how you can get testimonials without having your first client. Don't worry — there are ways to gather a couple of them right away.

- Offer free coaching sessions in exchange for a testimonial. This helps you get some practice under your belt as well.
- Talk to friends and family members whom you have helped in the past. It is okay to have testimonials from people you haven't coached as long as the testimonials are honest and authentic.
- Search through existing feedback and turn it into a testimonial. Look through your emails, previous job performance reviews and social media for any feedback you've had from peers, supervisors or professors. Testimonials do not necessarily have to be about your coaching at all. They can be a statement about your strengths, character or integrity. Make sure to contact the person to ask permission before using their words and name as a testimonial.

Hire a Coach

You may ask, "Why does a coach need a coach?"

If you are building a coaching business, you obviously believe in the power of coaching. If you don't, then you have chosen the wrong profession and you should stop reading right now.

Being a coach doesn't make you expert in everything. Perhaps you still need help managing your time, setting up and scaling your business, creating valuable content, or maybe you need accountability in the pursuit of your goals. Coaches still benefit from being coached. Because coaches cover almost every need imaginable, you can find a coach to help you with whatever you are struggling with.

Seeking outside help saves you time and frees you to focus on what you do best. If there is something you don't know which would take you months (or years) to figure out on your own, then the investment is worthwhile to get help from a professional.

Consider hiring a coach who specifically coaches other coaches. You can also join a mastermind group for extra accountability and to connect with like-minded people.

You may not be able to afford coaching and outside assistance when you first start your business. Contemplate the potential investment and whether it makes sense for you right now. If a personal coach is out of reach for the time being, join some free online communities. Surround yourself with people who are already succeeding at what you want to do.

Action Steps

1. Decide if you want to get certified. Do research on the various certification programs available and select one to pursue (if you choose). You do not have to complete a certification to start your practice.

2. Commit to a professional appearance every time you put your name or image out there. Take a fresh look at your website and social media profiles to ensure you are portraying the image of a professional coach. Make changes as necessary.

3. Decide which content strategy you want to pursue. As with everything, don't try to post content everywhere. Choose the avenues that speak to you and then focus your energies on those avenues. Don't spread yourself too thin.

4. Consider hiring a coach. List the pros and cons of hiring a coach at the beginning stages of your business and decide if the investment makes sense for you.

———

Positioning yourself as an expert is an ongoing strategy that will forever be important to your business. You need to dedicate time to creating and maintaining this image long-term. But even though it is ongoing, you can do a lot to set yourself up correctly from the beginning to establish yourself as a credible coach with expertise in your field. In the next chapter, you'll learn how to build your business by attracting a steady stream of ongoing clients.

14

ONGOING MARKETING

You've been hard at work setting up your coaching business and taking the necessary steps to start successfully. Now it is time to scale your business.

First, set up marketing systems so that you can attract a constant inflow of potential clients. Notice that we said "attract" instead of "look for." If you spend the time setting yourself up properly from the beginning, you will not fall into the common coaching pitfall of always being on the prowl for clients. Instead, everything you've worked so hard on will draw in eager customers like bees to honey.

The marketing strategies we discuss in this chapter are different from the outreach we covered in Chapter Eight. If you still have no or few clients, then we recommend you follow the steps in Chapter Eight and continue doing outreach. Then once you have at least five clients, you can start to think about how you're going to keep generating new business.

Get Clear on Your Message

Remember the work you did in Chapter Five to identify your niche and ideal client? Now you're going to put your findings to further use. If you can craft a clear message that speaks to your ideal client, you will create raving fans who are excited to invest in your programs. In order to do that, you have to get clear on what makes you different and answer the question, "Why you?" Why should your client hire you instead of another coach? Find out what your core message is and then put some compelling and unique language around it.

Start by revisiting your assignments in Chapter Five. Reread it all, slowly and out loud. Remember what drove you to your specific niche.

Next, you need to understand your why. Why do you want to coach in that specific niche? There is a famous quote by Simon Sinek that says, "People don't buy what you do. They buy why you do it." Any time a company or business has a strong mission and they stand behind something, it is powerful. You can harness that power in your business.

Knowing your why is key to attracting more of the right clients. The best copywriting contains three elements that come to life through your why.

- The pain your client currently feels.
- The pleasure they hope to experience.
- The benefit they receive from working with you.

Okay, let's home in on your why. If you've reread everything you wrote from Chapter Five, answers to the following three questions should come easily to you.

1. What do you love to do?

2. What impact do you desire to make?

3. Where do your natural talents lie?

Take your answers to those questions and craft a purpose statement. For example, here is Melissa's:

I work with high-achieving working mothers who are stuck behind self-doubt and fear to help them strengthen the relationship they have with themselves and create a world full of all of the abundance and success they could ever hope for.

And here is Sally's:

The purpose of my life is to be constantly learning and writing so that I can help people everywhere share their unique gifts and make money from home doing what they love.

When everything you write (website copy, emails, social media posts, etc.) comes from this message, you will have clients lining up to work with you.

Build Your Email List

We mentioned an opt-in incentive earlier on, it's time to revisit it. An email list is a critical piece of the client-attracting puzzle. People who have trusted you enough to give you their email address may trust you again in the future and invest in your services. You can publish a ton of content on your blogs and social media, but people may never see it. When you put your message out through email to your list, you are a lot more likely to get it in front of people's eyes.

But people typically don't just give out their email address for free. You need to incentivize them by offering something of value. While this is a little bit of extra work on your end, it is a good thing. If you provide something to your ideal client that helps him or her with a struggle, you are providing a sneak preview of what it is like to work with you.

Take another look at your ideal client. What can you give them for free that would bring immediate value to his or her life? Make sure it builds off your message and your specialty. For example, you might offer a short educational eBook, an inspirational audio recording, or a worksheet that helps them overcome a problem.

Set up an account with an email service provider. This enables you to capture your audience's names and email addresses in exchange for your opt-in incentive.

As a new coach starting out, you may be tempted to skip this expense, but we highly recommend you resist that urge. There are many affordable (and free) options to start with. The sooner you start building and nurturing your email list, the sooner you can begin selling your services.

Some popular email service providers are MailerLite, ConvertKit and Mailchimp. They all have excellent online articles to help you get started. If you're brand-new to email marketing, you can also follow Sally's step-by-step guide here: sallyannmiller.com/grow-your-email-list-convertkit.

Once you start building your email list, you can occasionally offer your products and services. But don't overwhelm their inbox with emails asking them to buy from you. Remember, you are not begging for clients. You are attracting them. Make sure your weekly emails are full of helpful content and news. Don't send repeated requests to jump on a discovery call without offering genuine value first.

You can also set up a sales funnel that is automatically sent out to new email subscribers. A sales funnel is a series of emails that gradually funnels readers down to an offer to work with you. You might start with a welcome email introducing yourself and letting them know what to expect. Follow this with two or three emails full of your best content and freebies. Then end with an email explaining your services and why they should buy from you. The idea behind a sales funnel is that you gradually build trust and prove your value before you try to sell. After your initial sales funnel, your weekly or biweekly newsletters take over.

Social Media

Using social media is another way to spread the word about what you do. Here are some strategies you can use to attract clients through social media:

1. Direct to Email List

Sharing content such as blog posts and landing pages through social media attracts people to your site, and then your opt-in incentive brings them onto your email list. Once these people subscribe to your email list, they go through your funnel (if you have one) and receive your newsletters. You build trust, and they may decide to invest in your coaching programs.

2. Sell Directly

You can also directly sell to your social media followers by posting special offers and invitations to discovery calls. This strategy works better as your social media following grows. Keep in mind that you should only try to sell, at most, in one out of every ten social media posts.

3. Live Video

What does work well is doing live videos through social media. In an interview he gave with Buzzfeed, Mark Zuckerberg said, "We're entering this new golden age of video. I wouldn't be surprised if you fast-forward five years and most of the content that people see on Facebook and are sharing on a day-to-day basis is video." Video, and especially live video, is a dominant social media trend. There is something raw and honest about going live that appeals to people. They get to see a behind-the-scenes look at how you operate. This builds trust over time.

4. Private Groups

This is one of the outreach methods we shared in Chapter Eight. Creating a private Facebook group can also form part of your ongoing marketing strategy. A lot of coaches and other entrepreneurs offer private Facebook groups to their followers. These groups serve as an exclusive community for your business and a place to connect with potential clients. The more you nurture your group and build trust, the more likely they are to purchase your services.

As we said before, don't bite off more than you can chew. Start out slowly with social media and experiment to see what works for your unique business. If you try everything at once, you'll succeed at nothing.

Paid Advertising

We don't suggest you start out using this method until you've mastered your message and proven its effectiveness with organic (free) options and social media. Advertising costs add up quickly. If you do it right, the payoff is large. If you do it wrong, it can be quite costly.

Here are a few places to advertise once you are ready for that step in your business:

- Social media — Facebook, Twitter, Pinterest, etc.
- Coupon companies — Groupon, Living Social
- Google Ads
- Local classifieds or newspaper
- Yelp

Facebook is a popular advertising platform for many coaches because it offers flexible ways to target your ideal audience. Advertising is an ongoing adventure that requires constant tweaking and optimizing. Before you start, come up with an initial budget. It takes some time and money to find the specific ad and targeting that converts the best.

We recommend you start paid advertising after your email list has over 1,000 subscribers. Perfect your message and prove that it's working and converting organically before investing money.

Complimentary Coaching

You can also attract new clients by offering free coaching sessions. When you give people a taste of your style and what they can expect from working with you, many will choose to buy. There are several different ways to offer complimentary coaching.

Free One-on-One Sessions

You can offer free one-on-one coaching sessions to potential clients and invite them to join your program at the end of your call. These phone calls can be strategy sessions or general Q&A calls. Make sure you limit the time you spend on free coaching but show your value. These free sessions are particularly valuable when you are starting out. You can use them to get testimonials and potentially sign your first paying client. Because individual sessions are time-consuming, limit the amount of free sessions you offer.

Free Assessments

You can offer free 20-minute assessments to potential clients and invite them to join your program at the end of the conversation. Assessments are quick calls where you look at something very specific and offer your opinion. For example, if you are a business coach, you could offer an assessment of your client's marketing strategy or sales script. The key is to tell them what is wrong and not how to fix it. The "how" is what they pay you for.

Free Webinars or Live Coaching

You can offer a free training seminar either through a webinar or live on Facebook or another social media platform. We love this option because you can prepare slides in advance and provide a lot of value. The last slides or talking points should ask people to sign up for a free discovery call with you to see what it would be like to work with you as their coach. These trainings work out well because they build trust and give you credibility. You can also save the videos and repurpose them later on.

Free Discovery Calls

Discovery calls aren't coaching calls at all. The purpose of a discovery call is to identify whether working together is a good fit for you and the client. Instead of coaching, you focus on the issues that the client is experiencing and then how your program can help. We talked more about discovery calls in Chapter Nine.

You can advertise and market your complimentary coaching offers through social media, email and paid advertisements.

Action Steps

1. Get clear on your message by answering the following three questions and crafting a "why" statement.

(a) What do you love to do?

(b) What impact do you desire to make?

(c) Where do your natural talents lie?

2. Research and choose an email service provider. Set up your account.

3. Create your free opt-in incentive and promote it on your website, social media and blog posts. Promote it anywhere and everywhere.

4. Determine which social media platforms you will use to promote your business and share valuable content. How will you invite clients into your business through these platforms?

5. Determine if you are ready to pay for advertising. If so set a budget to use while finding what works best for you.

6. Determine if you will offer any complimentary coaching. If you decide to, promote the offer in your email, on social media and by word of mouth.

We covered a lot of ground in this chapter. If you need to, take a break. This isn't a race. It's a journey to your amazing new career as a coach. There's just one more topic to cover. In the final chapter, you'll learn how to manage your time as you begin to scale your business.

15

SCALING YOUR BUSINESS

Congratulations! You now have your own coaching business, and your doors are open. You may have already signed your first paying clients. There is nowhere to go from here except up. Depending on your income goals and aspirations, you may desire to scale your business and earn more money as a coach. In this chapter we share ways to scale your business and create a dream coaching business that fits your life and serves your clients.

But first, a word of caution: as a new business owner, you have a lot to learn. It is tempting to try to learn it all at once or spend every waking minute working on your business. But remember, one of the perks of owning your own business is the freedom that comes with it. Don't let this new adventure completely take over your life — as tempting as that may be in the beginning.

Scale Correctly

Protect your time by putting the foundational building blocks in place to scale correctly. Look at your coaching programs and models. Are they set up to scale?

If you are only selling one-on-one sessions, you have two choices:

1. Increase prices

2. Increase the number of clients

You can and should raise your prices over time, but you will reach a threshold where people will not pay more for your services. You can take on more clients, but there are only so many hours in a day. In order to give your clients the service they deserve, you should not coach more than you can emotionally and mentally handle. Therefore, one-on-one sessions do not scale well.

If you are selling group packages and online courses, you are in a better position to keep growing your business income. You may also choose to set up a subscription-based service or start a mastermind group. All these options allow you to serve more clients in fewer hours. Your potential income is limitless once you start offering scalable programs.

Manage Your Calendar

It is important to manage your calendar as a coach. There is a lot more that goes into the day-to-day activities than just coaching, including:

- Preparation for coaching calls
- Coaching calls
- Marketing/advertising
- Maintaining your online presence (social media, live videos, guest posts/podcast interviews, blog posts)
- Email list nurturing
- Facebook group nurturing
- Brand building and maintaining
- Discovery and sales calls
- Income and expense tracking
- Product and services updates and improvements

If you don't make time on your calendar for these activities, they may drop off your radar or keep you up working until the wee hours of the night.

So how do you fit it all in without working 60-plus hours per week?

The answer is simple.

You look for the activities that are directly tied to the growth and prosperity of your business. Anything else is a distraction for you, and therefore should not be a priority. For example, coaching your clients and holding discovery calls are paramount to your business and must be handled as a priority. Posting to your Facebook page may be more distracting than profitable. However, just because something is a distraction doesn't mean it isn't necessary. For example, bookkeeping won't help you land more clients, but it is essential.

Eliminate/Automate/Delegate

Once you determine which activities are most important, try to eliminate, automate or delegate the rest. If you are looking to scale your business, you cannot do it all.

First, look for tasks you can eliminate. Are there activities on your to-do list that add little to no value? For example, if you spend time updating your Twitter account daily, but aren't generating any clients through Twitter, then it isn't worth your time.

Next, automate as many activities as possible. There are so many cool gadgets out there to automate tasks in your business. Your email service provider can be set up to automate emails, funnels, and even sales. Your calendar can be automated. Your social media can be automated. A lot of things can be set up to operate on autopilot. So you can set it and forget it. Automate as much as you can in your business. Any time you find yourself doing a mindless task repeatedly, look for a way to automate it.

Finally, you can consider delegating tasks in your business. This frees you to focus your energy on the critical tasks without getting burned out or overwhelmed. Outsourcing allows you to grow quicker and make that money back. Virtual assistance is available for almost everything. You can outsource tasks ranging from social media to website design to bookkeeping and taxes.

Plan Your Days

"Success doesn't just happen. It is planned."

— ANONYMOUS

In most cases, what makes successful people successful isn't intelligence, looks or wealth. It is the fact that they know how to manage their time. The reason so many new businesses fail early on is that people don't focus on the right things. Many new business owners live reactively instead of proactively.

You've spent all this time and effort setting up your new coaching business. Don't let it fail simply because you waste your time. Planning doesn't have to be complicated either.

Here are some simple tips:

1. Determine the top priorities of your business and personal life.

2. Set goals for your business and personal life (we'll talk more about how to do this later in this chapter).

3. Make sure you set aside time every day to work on your priorities and goals.

4. Plan your week each Sunday. Go through your daily plan the night before.

5. Keep a running list of tasks. Try to break these tasks up into ten-minute activities. If you find yourself with extra time (waiting for a doctor's appointment, early to a meeting, etc.), use that time to knock out a task or two instead of browsing social media.

6. Every time something new comes up, ask yourself: "Does this activity align with my business or personal goals?" If it doesn't, politely say, "No, thank you." If you can apply this filter to your business and life, you avoid

wasting your time on activities and tasks that do not move you forward.

Map Out Your Ideal Week

Get everything on your calendar! A calendar is a tool that can save you many hours per week if you use it correctly.

The best way to be productive and efficient with your time is to map out an ideal week with set themes. Then you can schedule your tasks within those pre-designated time chunks.

For example, perhaps you handle your team meetings on Mondays. Tuesdays are for content creation and creative work. Wednesdays through Fridays are set aside for coaching calls and sales calls. Or even better, maybe Fridays are set aside for family time.

Once you have your daily themes set up, break your days into large chunks for dedicated deep work (uninterrupted work). Batch similar tasks for increased productivity. Don't forget to include time for goal setting, continued learning, exercise and self-reflection.

The week that you have mapped out can be transferred to your calendar. You can even color-code your calendar by category.

While it is not realistic to assume that you will always be able to maintain this schedule, it gives you a template to work from so that you can quickly get back on track.

Set Goals and Maintain Progress

We've already mentioned the importance of goals. It's worth spending some time talking about how to set goals that help you achieve the success you deserve.

Goals help you stay focused and provide you with a way to measure your progress and growth. But how do you set the right goals?

As you set your goals, it is important to ensure each one aligns with your values and life priorities. For example, if you have a goal to get certified as a coach in 30 days (which will require you working long hours), but spending time with your young children is a priority, you may need to reevaluate your goal.

You should also set goals in different areas of your life. If you set all your goals for your new business, the other areas of your life may suffer.

Once you get your goals written out, you need to manage your time so that you make consistent daily progress without getting overwhelmed or distracted.

It is so easy to get caught up in information overload in the world we live in today. However, you must guard your time and focus your efforts on what matters most in your life and business.

For more help on setting goals, visit the free bonus area here: sallyannmiller.com/coachbook. We have a free *Turn Your Dreams Into Goals* eBook that will help you set powerful goals in your business and life.

Action Steps

1. Determine which tasks in your business can be eliminated, automated or delegated.

2. Write out specific goals for your business and determine how you will measure your progress.

3. Create an ideal schedule for your week and load it into your calendar.

16

CONCLUSION

You made it. Congratulations on reaching the end!

We've packed a lot of information into this book. You may need time to digest the content before taking the first steps. That's okay. This is your journey and it's important to follow your own path.

Having said that, if you're committed to becoming a life coach, don't wait too long. If you delay, you may never discover your true calling. Clarity comes from action, and action drives results.

In this book, we've provided the exact steps to become a life coach and attract your first paying clients. We also shared strategies to help you scale your business to six figures and beyond. Follow these steps and see where they lead you. The next few months may literally change your life.

To close, I want to offer you some final words of encouragement. Embarking on a new career is never easy. I urge you to be gentle on yourself. Treat this as a voyage of self-discovery.

We've crammed it full of free goodies for you. And if there's anything missing, you can always email me. I'll point you in the right direction. Plus, when you sign up, I'll invite you to join my private Facebook group where you can get more support and free training with me.

Wherever you go next, I wish you all the best. May you dream big, take action, and live an amazing life.

EXCERPT: MAKE MONEY FROM ONLINE COURSES

The knowledge industry is booming, and online learning is especially popular. According to a research report by Global Market Insights, the e-learning market will be worth over $300 billion by 2025. Given recent events, the eventual market size will probably exceed this prediction. Early in 2020, the COVID-19 pandemic led many people to move from in-person to online study. In response to this shift, the world expanded its capability and appetite for digital learning.

We live in a time when anyone can learn anything from the comfort of their own home. You no longer need to sign up for classes at your local community college. Anyone with internet access can register for an online course and have instant access to new information.

For the entrepreneur, this has created immense opportunity. Online courses are cheap to design and deliver. There's no limit to the number of students you can serve. Through online marketing, you can reach a global audience and impact millions of people while working from home.

However, course creation doesn't come without challenges. The low barrier of entry means that anyone can throw together a digital program and offer it for sale. Competition is significant, and the quality of courses is variable. Consumers who have been exposed to questionable online products and marketing techniques are wary about who they give their money to.

The days when you could be first to market with a new online product are long over. If you want to profit from your course, you must commit to building and selling the best offering you can.

As a course creator, you also have a myriad of technical tools at your disposal. While this may seem like an advantage, it can be overwhelming. Should you create an email course or video-based program? How should you host and deliver your content? What marketing tools and methods are most effective? How can you avoid launching your course to crickets?

This book answers all these questions and more. In these pages, you will discover exactly how to create an online course people want to buy. You will also learn the exact steps to launch your new product with maximum impact. You have knowledge to share with the world. With the help of this book, you can start earning from your first course in less than three months.

Between them, the authors of this book have sold short email-based courses, high-end video programs, and membership sites. They have made mistakes and learned from them. They have mastered the tools of course creation, implemented profitable sales funnels, and delighted students with their innovative offerings. They understand what contemporary course buyers want and how to market digital products without wasting time and money.

However, course creation isn't a get-rich-quick scheme. Creating and selling your first digital product takes passion and dedication. You must build a solution people want, then commit to sharing it with the students you are destined to help. You must devote yourself to serving your audience and providing the highest level of product and support. And you must never stop marketing.

If you're willing to do these things, then you can turn your knowledge into a profitable business.

Why Offer an Online Course?

Before we get started, ask yourself whether creating a course is right for you and your business. Is this something you even want to do? To help you decide, the following are the most common reasons why people sell online courses. Do any of these resonate with you?

For Leveraged Income

Once you create your course and work out the marketing and delivery kinks, you can automate many aspects of the selling process. While it's not completely hands-off, your income potential is unlimited. With minimal additional effort, you can sell hundreds, even thousands, of copies of your digital product.

However, don't be lured by the promise of passive income. You still need to maintain your course and provide customer service. In today's competitive market, the most successful course creators are constantly improving their content for new and existing customers.

To Monetize a Small Audience

With an online course, you can start making money even if you have zero or a handful of followers. This book shows you how to sell the first version of your course and then grow your audience once you have a profitable idea. It also teaches you how to keep selling your product so that you can build up a sustainable income.

To Be Seen as an Expert

Building a course around a topic shows your expertise in the subject. Having a course increases your authority and credibility. This leads to more opportunities in your niche. For example, you can offer a short course as an entry product for new customers. Then pitch higher ticket services once people have enjoyed your initial offering.

As a course creator, you establish yourself as someone who is making a difference in your niche. You demonstrate your unique perspective and passion for your topic. And people will be drawn to find out more about you and what you provide.

To Grow an Engaged Audience

As an online business owner, you want to connect with your tribe and grow your audience. Online courses can help you do that. As you market your product, you present yourself as an expert who can solve a key problem for your target audience.

Students who complete your course build a relationship with you. They get to know who you are and your teaching style. Your students become your most loyal followers. These are the people who go on to buy your other products and services.

Marketing an online course is a proven way to expand your email list and create a loyal fanbase. We dive deep into how to build a tribe in chapter eight and chapter nine of this book.

To Help Others

People who create online courses often have the heart of a teacher. They enjoy breaking problems down into bite-sized chunks and passing their knowledge on to others. An online course allows you to help a larger audience, rather than working with people one-on-one.

You know your potential students better than anyone else. And only you can make the perfect course for them. By creating your own product—instead of selling someone else's—you develop the ideal solution for your tribe.

In short, online courses expand your ability to help others in a meaningful way. And for many, that is reason enough to create an online course.

These are not the only drivers to build a digital product, but if you want to succeed, you must be clear on why you're doing this. You will face obstacles on your journey and your reasons will motivate you to keep moving forward.

So take time now to decide on your why. Write it down. Keep it close. And whenever you're feeling doubts, pull it out and read it.

11 Steps to Course Success

Having a clear purpose prepares you for success, but motivation is not all you need. You must also follow a process.

There are thousands of ways to bring your first product to market. All of them can work, though some are more effective than others. The problem is that most new course creators get lost pursuing too many ideas. They spread themselves too thin and fail to gain traction.

The answer is to stick with one system. This book teaches you one such process. It is based on the authors' experience in the online space. It isn't a restrictive formula; you can adapt it to suit you and your audience. But there are some key elements you must not skip.

The system is designed to ensure your idea is viable before you invest your valuable time and money. You will start by selecting a course topic. Then you test your idea by selling a limited version of your course. We call this your Minimum Viable Course (MVC). Once your first students complete your MVC, you can build and launch the final version of your product.

There are 11 steps in total:

1. Select a Topic

2. Define Your MVC

3. Test Your Idea

4. Pick a Platform

5. Outline Your Course

6. Create Your MVC

7. Refine Your Course

8. Build Your Tribe

9. Engage Your Tribe

10. Update Your Sales Page

11. Re-Launch Your Course

In the following chapters, we walk through each of these steps one at a time. Follow the directions and complete the action steps. Do this and you will make money from your first online course. This system works, but only if you commit to developing and selling the best product you can. Do you have what it takes to make money as a course creator? Let's find out.

Keep Reading *Make Money From Online Courses* – available in online bookstores now!

www.ingramcontent.com/pod-product-compliance
Lightning Source LLC
Chambersburg PA
CBHW081817200326
41597CB00023B/4282